Hey there, future survivors!

Welcome to "The End of the World: Survival Guide, Trivia and Fact Book for the End of the World." Are you ready to embark on the wildest adventure ever? Imagine a world where everything has changed, and it's up to you to survive and thrive. Whether it's dodging zombies, building a bunker, or navigating through nuclear fallout, this book has got you covered.

Why did we create this guide? Because who doesn't love a good challenge? Plus, learning how to survive the end of the world is just plain cool! You'll become the ultimate survival expert, ready for anything life throws your way.

In this book, you'll discover how to build the safest bunkers, find out what to do during a nuclear fallout, and even learn how to fend off zombies (yes, really!). But that's not all – you'll also learn how to form your own survival group, build an outpost, and create a brand-new society from scratch. Imagine setting up your own trading system, creating laws, and growing a community garden. It's like being the ruler of your very own kingdom!

And don't worry, we've packed this guide with fun facts and trivia to keep things interesting. Did you know there's a bunker that can fit over 5,000 people? Or that the hottest place on Earth is called Death Valley? You'll find these and other awesome facts throughout the book.

So, grab your backpack and let's get started. The end of the world doesn't stand a chance against you!

Table of Contents

When the world goes wild, the wild get creative!

Chapter 1: The Bunker

The unthinkable has happened: news reports flood in about escalating global tensions and the looming threat of nuclear war. You and your friends, determined to be prepared for any eventuality, decide to build a nuclear bunker. This isn't just about survival; it's about creating a safe haven where you can weather the storm together. The project quickly becomes a blend of practicality and creativity, as you turn your backyard into a construction site for your underground fortress.

The first step is choosing the perfect location. After much deliberation, you settle on a spot in your backyard that offers both concealment and easy access. With shovels and determination, you begin digging, transforming the earth beneath your feet into the foundation of your bunker. The process is grueling but also incredibly rewarding, as each layer of dirt removed brings you closer to your goal. You and your friends take turns, encouraging each other and sharing the excitement of building something that could save your lives.

Once the digging is complete, it's time to fortify your bunker. You gather materials like concrete, steel, and wood, turning your vision into reality. The construction process is both challenging and fun, as you solve problems and innovate solutions together. You design and build the interior, ensuring it has all the essentials: food and water storage, sleeping areas, and even some entertainment options to keep morale high. The bunker becomes a symbol of your resourcefulness and teamwork.

Living in the bunker, even just for drills, is a unique experience. You establish routines to keep busy and maintain a sense of normalcy. From playing games and reading books to working on DIY projects like bunker decor, you find ways to make the confined space feel like home. The bunker, once a grim necessity, turns into a place of safety and camaraderie. Through it all, you learn that preparation and teamwork are your greatest assets, making even the darkest scenarios manageable with the right mindset.

Preparing for the worst makes every moment of peace even sweeter."

Designing and Building a Bunker

Structural Integrity

Building a nuclear war bunker isn't just about digging a hole and calling it a day. Think of it as constructing your very own underground fortress! You'll need materials that can withstand blasts, radiation, and fallout. Reinforced concrete is your best friend here. It's strong, durable, and can absorb radiation. If you're feeling fancy, add some steel rebar for extra strength. Remember, your bunker walls should be at least three feet thick to provide adequate protection.

Ventilation Systems

Ventilation is crucial unless you fancy the idea of turning your bunker into a giant, underground sauna. Install a HEPA filtration system to filter out radioactive particles and other contaminants. Activated carbon filters can also help eliminate harmful gases. And don't forget to add manual crank ventilation as a backup. It's the 21st century, but let's be real—technology can fail, and a good old hand-crank system can be a lifesaver (literally).

Layout and Space Utilization

Space in a bunker is as precious as a Wi-Fi signal in a teenager's bedroom. Design your layout to maximize every inch. Use foldable furniture, bunk beds, and multi-functional items. Think about how submarines or RVs utilize space. Have designated areas for sleeping, eating, and storing supplies. A well-organized bunker not only boosts efficiency but keeps morale high.

"A well-prepared bunker is like a cozy underground club, minus the cell service."

Waterproofing and Insulation

A leaky bunker is no better than a broken umbrella in a rainstorm. Waterproofing your bunker is essential. Use waterproof concrete sealant and install proper drainage systems to keep water out. For insulation, consider spray foam or rigid foam boards to maintain a stable temperature. It'll keep you cozy in the winter and cool in the summer. Remember, comfort equals survival.

Entrance and Exit

Your bunker needs a secure entrance and exit—think of it as the gate to your castle. Use heavy-duty, blast-resistant doors that can be securely locked from the inside. Have at least two exits in case one gets blocked. Conceal your entrance with natural landscaping or structures to avoid unwanted attention. After all, you don't want to invite every curious squirrel or, worse, desperate human to your secret lair.

Power Supply

Electricity is a luxury you don't want to skip. Install solar panels above ground with battery storage below to harness and store energy. Generators can provide backup power, but make sure you have enough fuel to keep them running. Consider wind turbines if you live in a windy area. Remember, you'll need power for lighting, ventilation, cooking, and charging your essential gadgets—like your all-important zombie apocalypse video game collection.

Water Supply

Water is life, and in a bunker, you need a reliable source. Install a deep well with a hand pump or an electric pump connected to your power supply. Store bottled water as a backup, aiming for at least one gallon per person per day. Consider a rainwater harvesting system with proper filtration to collect and purify water. Remember, a well-hydrated survivor is a happy survivor.

Waste Management

Dealing with waste in a confined space is no fun, but it's necessary. Install a composting toilet or a chemical toilet to manage human waste. For greywater (from washing dishes or bathing), set up a simple filtration system to separate solids and purify the water. Keep waste management systems well-maintained to prevent any unpleasant odors or health hazards.

Food Storage

You can't survive on canned beans alone, although they're a good start. Dedicate a section of your bunker for food storage. Stockpile non-perishable items like canned goods, dried foods, and vacuum-sealed meals. Consider growing your own food with an indoor hydroponic or aquaponic system. This not only provides fresh produce but keeps you busy and adds some greenery to your underground life.

Communication Systems

Staying connected to the outside world is crucial, even if it's just to hear the latest news or SOS signals. Install a ham radio and ensure you know how to use it. Keep a supply of charged batteries and consider a hand-crank radio as a backup. Satellite phones can also be useful. Communication systems keep you informed and can be a lifeline in emergencies.

Building your own nuclear bunker is a mix of practicality and creativity. It's about being prepared for the worst while making the best of your underground paradise. Stay quirky, stay prepared, and remember, the key to survival is a combination of solid planning and a good sense of humor.

"In the bunker of life, stockpile laughter and friendship as much as food."

Crazy Facts

- Deep Freeze Bunkers: Did you know there's a bunker in Norway called the Svalbard Global Seed Vault? It stores over a million seed samples from around the world to preserve plant diversity in case of a global catastrophe!
- Blast from the Past: The oldest known bunkers date back to ancient times. The Romans built underground refuges called "catacombs" which served as hiding places during wars!
- Presidential Bunker: The U.S. president has a secret bunker called the Presidential Emergency Operations Center (PEOC) located beneath the White House. It's designed to keep the president safe during national emergencies.
- Luxury Bunkers: Some modern bunkers are more like luxury hotels. They come with swimming pools, theaters, gyms, and even spas! Imagine surviving the apocalypse in style!
- Meteor Defense: Besides nuclear fallout, some bunkers are designed to withstand meteor strikes. Scientists believe this could help protect humanity from an unexpected space rock collision.
- Underground Cities: There are entire underground cities like Derinkuyu in Turkey, which could house up to 20,000 people! These ancient cities had everything from schools to stables, all built underground.
- Bunker Parties: During the Cold War, some families in the U.S. held "bunker parties" to practice what they would do in

case of a nuclear attack. They stocked their bunkers with games, snacks, and even comic books to keep morale high.

- Secret Soviet Bunkers: In Russia, there are numerous secret bunkers built during the Soviet era. Some are so well-hidden that their exact locations are still classified!
- Animal Bunkers: Some wealthy pet owners have built bunkers specifically for their furry friends, complete with dog parks, cat trees, and lots of treats to keep them happy during tough times.
- Future Bunkers: Scientists are designing futuristic bunkers with hydroponic farms that grow food using just water and light. These could be essential for long-term survival underground.

Waterproofing and Insulation

A leaky bunker is no better than a broken umbrella in a rainstorm. Waterproofing your bunker is essential. Use waterproof concrete sealant and install proper drainage systems to keep water out. For insulation, consider spray foam or rigid foam boards to maintain a stable temperature. It'll keep you cozy in the winter and cool in the summer. Remember, comfort equals survival.

Crazy Fact: Did you know there's an underground city in Turkey called Derinkuyu that could house up to 20,000 people? It had everything from schools to stables, all built underground!

Countries with the Most Bunkers in the World

1. Switzerland:

- Fun Fact: Switzerland is famous for its extensive network of bunkers, with enough capacity to shelter its entire population. The Swiss government has a long-standing policy of ensuring every citizen has access to a fallout shelter. Many homes and apartment buildings come equipped with private bunkers, and there are public shelters in almost every community.

2. Russia:

- Fun Fact: Russia has a vast array of bunkers dating back to the Cold War era. These include elaborate underground facilities in major cities like Moscow, designed to protect government officials and civilians alike. Some of these bunkers are rumored to be massive, with the ability to sustain life for extended periods.

3. United States:

- Fun Fact: The United States has numerous bunkers spread across the country, many of which are remnants of the Cold War. The most famous include the Cheyenne Mountain Complex in Colorado, which houses the North American Aerospace Defense Command (NORAD). Private bunker building has also seen a resurgence, with companies offering custom-built survival bunkers.

4. Sweden:

- Fun Fact: Sweden has a comprehensive network of bunkers, originally built during the Cold War to protect against nuclear attacks. Many of these bunkers have been maintained and updated over the years. The Swedish government actively promotes preparedness, and bunkers are a common feature in residential buildings and public spaces.

5. North Korea:

- Fun Fact: North Korea is known for its extensive network of underground bunkers and tunnels. These structures are designed to protect the regime and military assets from potential attacks. The country's mountainous terrain has been heavily utilized for creating these secretive and often highly fortified underground facilities.

The Birth of the Bunker Boom

1. Cold War Tensions

Imagine the world as a giant playground, but instead of kids playing tag, you've got two big kids—let's call them the United States and the Soviet Union—having the world's most intense staring contest. This period of geopolitical tension from 1947 to 1991 is known as the Cold War. Unlike a typical playground squabble, these two weren't just arguing over toys; they were armed with enough nuclear weapons to turn the sandbox into a desert.

2. Nuclear Arms Race: The Ultimate "My Bike is Cooler" Contest

The Cold War was like the ultimate "my bike is cooler than your bike" contest, but instead of bikes, it was nuclear missiles. Both sides raced to build bigger and better weapons, each trying to outdo the other. This arms race created a palpable sense of fear worldwide. People wondered if, or when, someone might push the big red button, launching the world into nuclear chaos.

3. Duck and Cover: The Ultimate Hide-and-Seek

Just like playing hide-and-seek, people were told to "duck and cover" if they saw the bright flash of a nuclear explosion. Schools even had drills where kids practiced hiding under their desks. While it might seem silly to think a desk could protect you from a nuclear blast, it was all part of trying to be prepared for the worst. Imagine practicing your hiding skills, hoping you'd never have to use them for real!

4. Bunker Building: The New Underground Clubhouse

In response to the looming threat, countries around the world started digging—literally. Governments began constructing bunkers like kids building secret clubhouses, but these were made to withstand bombs, not just keep out nosy siblings. Reinforced concrete, steel doors, and air filtration systems turned these underground hideouts into mini-fortresses. Families even built their own bunkers in backyards, turning the ultimate DIY project into a survival necessity.

5. Global Bunker Boom: Keeping Cool Under Pressure

This bunker-building frenzy wasn't just about staying safe; it was also about staying cool under pressure. Countries competed to see who could build the safest, most advanced bunkers. Switzerland became the world's bunker-building champion, with enough shelters to protect its entire population. The Cold War might have been a time of great fear, but it also showcased human ingenuity and the desire to protect what matters most.

Crazy Facts

Secret Underground Cities: Beneath Paris lies an extensive network of tunnels and bunkers known as the Catacombs. While originally created as limestone quarries, these tunnels were later used to house millions of human bones and have served as hiding places during times of war.

Underground Bunker Hotels: In Germany, there are former Cold War bunkers that have been transformed into luxury hotels. Guests can experience what it's like to stay in a bunker, complete with high-end amenities and historical tours.

Bunker with a Swimming Pool: The Oppidum in the Czech Republic is known as the largest billionaire bunker in the world. It includes a swimming pool, garden, cinema, and even a wine cellar, blending luxury with survival preparedness.

Do-It-Yourself Bunker Kits: In the U.S., some companies offer DIY bunker kits that come with all the materials and instructions you need to build your own underground shelter. It's like a giant Lego set, but for survival!

World War II Relics: During World War II, the British government built bunkers called Anderson shelters in backyards across the country. These simple, corrugated iron structures saved countless lives during air raids.

Bunkers for Data: Some modern bunkers are designed to protect data instead of people. Companies like Google and Microsoft have massive underground data centers to protect critical information from natural and man-made disasters.

Animal Bunkers: During the Cold War, the U.S. government built bunkers to protect livestock from nuclear fallout. These bunkers had special ventilation systems to keep the animals safe and healthy.

Moon Bunkers: Scientists are exploring the idea of building bunkers on the moon! These lunar bunkers could protect astronauts from cosmic radiation and extreme temperatures, making long-term moon missions possible.

Celebrity Bunkers: Some Hollywood celebrities have invested in private bunkers. These luxurious shelters are equipped with everything from gyms and spas to movie theaters, ensuring they can ride out any disaster in style.

Subterranean Farms: In addition to survival bunkers, some underground spaces are being used for farming. These "vertical farms" use LED lights and hydroponic systems to grow crops year-round, regardless of surface conditions.

Historic Hideaways: During the Cold War, the U.S. government built a secret bunker under the Greenbrier Resort in West Virginia. It was intended to house Congress in the event of a nuclear attack and remained a secret for over 30 years.

Bunkers in Popular Culture: Bunkers have appeared in numerous movies and TV shows, often depicted as the last refuge during apocalyptic events. For example, in the movie "10 Cloverfield Lane," a bunker plays a central role in the survival of the characters.

Ice Bunkers: In the Arctic, researchers have created bunkers built into the ice to store seeds from around the world. This Global Seed Vault, also known as the "Doomsday Vault," ensures the preservation of diverse plant species in case of global disasters.

Mini Bunkers for Pets: Some pet lovers have created mini bunkers designed specifically for their furry friends. These pet-sized shelters are equipped with ventilation, food supplies, and cozy bedding to keep pets safe during emergencies.

Stockpiling Supplies: Your Bunker Shopping List

Food and Water: Stay Nourished and Hydrated

Water:

- Storage: Aim for at least 1 gallon of water per person per day. For a 2-week supply for a family of four, that's 56 gallons.
- Purification: Water purification tablets, a portable water filter (like a LifeStraw), and bleach (for emergency disinfection—use 8 drops per gallon).

Non-Perishable Foods:

- Canned Goods: Vegetables, fruits, beans, meats, and soups.
- Dry Goods: Rice, pasta, oatmeal, powdered milk, and instant coffee.
- Snacks: Granola bars, nuts, dried fruits, and jerky.
- Emergency Rations: MREs (Meals Ready-to-Eat) and freeze-dried meals.

Medical Supplies: Be Ready for Anything

First Aid Kit:

- Adhesive bandages (various sizes)
- Sterile gauze pads and medical tape
- Antiseptic wipes and hydrogen peroxide
- Scissors, tweezers, and a digital thermometer
- Instant cold packs

Prescription Medications:

- 30-day supply of any prescription medications
- Pain relievers (ibuprofen, acetaminophen)
- Allergy medications (antihistamines)

Protective Gear:

- Disposable gloves and face masks
- N95 respirators
- Eye protection (goggles)
- Hand sanitizer and disinfectant wipes

Tools and Equipment: Keep Things Running Smoothly

Maintenance and Repair:

- Multi-tool or Swiss Army knife
- Duct tape and super glue
- Wrenches, screwdrivers, and pliers

- Nails, screws, and a hammer
- Flashlights and extra batteries

Everyday Tasks:

- Solar or battery-powered lanterns
- Manual can opener
- Fire extinguisher
- Battery-operated radio
- Waterproof matches and lighters

Sanitation and Hygiene: Stay Clean and Healthy

Toilets and Waste Disposal:

- Portable camping toilet or composting toilet
- Heavy-duty garbage bags
- Toilet paper and biodegradable wipes

Hygiene Supplies:

- Hand soap and body wash
- Toothbrushes and toothpaste
- Feminine hygiene products
- Towels and washcloths
- Shampoo and conditioner

Cleaning Supplies:

- Bleach and disinfectant sprays
- Mop and bucket
- Broom and dustpan
- Sponges and cleaning cloths

With this comprehensive shopping list, you'll be well-prepared to stockpile your bunker and ensure that you have everything you need to stay nourished, healthy, and comfortable during any extended stay. Just think of it as prepping for the ultimate camping trip—except you're underground and ready for anything!

Managing Energy and Power: Keeping Your Bunker Operational

In a well-prepared bunker, energy management is the difference between surviving in the dark and thriving in the light."

Power Sources: Fueling Your Underground Fortress

Generators:

- Gasoline Generators: Reliable and powerful, but require a steady fuel supply. Store gasoline safely and use stabilizers to prolong shelf life.
- Propane Generators: Cleaner burning than gasoline and the fuel stores indefinitely. Ensure you have enough propane tanks.
- Diesel Generators: Efficient for long-term use and diesel fuel has a longer shelf life compared to gasoline.

Solar Panels:

- Rooftop Solar Panels: Install panels above ground to harness the power of the sun. Connect them to a battery bank for storage.
- Portable Solar Kits: Useful for smaller needs and can be repositioned for optimal sun exposure.

Battery Banks:

- Deep Cycle Batteries: Store energy from solar panels or generators. Use batteries designed for repeated charging and discharging.
- Lithium-Ion Batteries: More efficient and longer-lasting than traditional lead-acid batteries, though more expensive.

Energy Conservation: Prioritize and Preserve

Lighting:

- LED Lights: Use LED bulbs as they consume less power and have a longer lifespan.
- Motion Sensor Lights: Install in less frequently used areas to save energy.

Ventilation:

- Manual Crank Ventilation: Use hand-crank ventilators as a backup to electric systems.
- Timed Ventilation: Program ventilation systems to run at intervals, reducing constant power consumption.

Communication:

- Efficient Devices: Use energy-efficient communication devices like radios and tablets.
- Scheduled Use: Limit usage to essential times to conserve battery life.

General Tips:

- Unplug When Not in Use: Disconnect appliances and devices when they're not needed to avoid phantom loads.
- Insulate Properly: Good insulation reduces the need for heating and cooling, saving energy.
- Charge During Peak Sunlight: If using solar power, charge devices and batteries during peak sunlight hours.

Backup Systems: Stay Prepared

Redundancy:

- Multiple Generators: Have more than one generator in case one fails.

- Diverse Power Sources: Use a combination of solar, wind, and fuel-based generators for flexibility.

Maintenance:

- Regular Checks: Perform routine maintenance on all power systems to ensure they are in working order.
- Spare Parts: Keep a stock of spare parts such as filters, spark plugs, and fuses.

Repair Kits:

- Tool Kit: Include tools specifically for repairing electrical and mechanical components.
- Instruction Manuals: Have manuals for all equipment to guide you through troubleshooting and repairs.

"Powering your underground sanctuary requires ingenuity and foresight; every watt conserved is a step towards sustainable survival."

Fun Bunker Activities

Staying in a bunker might sound a bit grim, but with the right activities, it can be a blast! Here are some fun bunker activities to keep you entertained and your spirits high. We've got ideas for hanging out with a buddy and for those times when you're flying solo.

Fun with a Buddy

1. Board Game Bonanza: Grab your favorite board games and challenge your buddy to a marathon session. Whether it's classics like Monopoly and Scrabble or intense strategy games like Risk, there's nothing like some friendly competition to pass the time. Keep a scoreboard and see who emerges as the ultimate bunker champion!

2. Bunker Olympics: Create your own mini-Olympics with events like paper airplane flying contests, indoor obstacle courses, or a scavenger hunt around the bunker. Award medals (made from aluminum foil) to the winners and celebrate with a mini closing ceremony.

3. Movie Night Madness: Set up a cozy movie corner with blankets and pillows, and have a movie marathon. Pick a theme, like superhero flicks, animated classics, or even a zombie apocalypse series to stay in the survival spirit. Don't forget the popcorn!

4. Cooking Challenges: Use your stored food supplies to have a cooking competition. Who can make the tastiest meal with canned beans and freeze-dried vegetables? Get creative with your ingredients and pretend you're on a survival cooking show. Bon appétit!

5. DIY Crafts and Projects: Gather your art supplies and work on DIY projects together. Make friendship bracelets, paint a mural on one of the bunker walls, or even build models out of whatever materials you have. It's a great way to stay creative and bond with your buddy.

Fun Solo Activities

1. Bunker Book Club: Dive into that stack of books you've been meaning to read. Create a reading nook with some comfy cushions and a good light source. Keep a journal to jot down your thoughts and favorite quotes from each book. Bonus points if you share your reviews with your bunker buddies!

2. Exercise Routine: Staying active is crucial, even in a bunker. Design your own workout routine with exercises like push-ups, sit-ups, and jumping jacks. Use cans or water bottles as weights for strength training. Keep track of your progress and set goals to stay motivated.

3. Creative Writing: Channel your inner author and write stories, poems, or even a bunker diary. Imagine different scenarios and adventures outside the bunker or write about your experiences and thoughts while in hiding. Who knows? You might write the next great post-apocalyptic novel!

4. Puzzle Time: Pull out that jigsaw puzzle and get to work! It's a perfect solo activity that can keep you busy for hours. If puzzles aren't your thing, try crossword puzzles, Sudoku, or brainteasers to keep your mind sharp.

Radio Station Setup

"Radio is the theater of the mind; television is the theater of the mindless." – Steve Allen

Why Set Up a Radio Station?

1. Entertainment: Music and stories can lift spirits and break the monotony of bunker life. A radio station provides endless entertainment options, from playing your favorite songs to hosting engaging shows.

2. Communication: Keeping everyone informed about bunker updates or sharing important news from the outside world is essential. Your radio station can serve as a communication hub.

3. Creativity: Running a radio station lets you unleash your creativity. You can come up with different show ideas, create playlists, and even practice your DJ voice.

4. Bonding: A radio station can bring everyone together. Whether you're tuning in to listen or taking turns hosting shows, it's a great way to strengthen bonds with your bunker mates.

How to Set Up Your Bunker Radio Station

Gather Your Supplies:

- Vinyl records and CDs: Organize them by genre or mood.
- A record player and CD player: Ensure they are in good working condition.
- A microphone: A hairbrush can serve as a pretend mic, or use an actual microphone if available.
- Speakers: Good quality speakers to broadcast your shows.

Organize Your Music: Create playlists for different times of the day:

- Morning Wake-Up Tunes: Energize your day with upbeat tracks.
- Afternoon Jams: Keep the momentum going with fun, lively music.
- Evening Chill-Out Tracks: Wind down with relaxing tunes.

Set Up Your Broadcasting Studio:

- Find a cozy corner of the bunker to set up your station. Arrange your record player, CD player, and microphone. Decorate the area to make it feel like a real studio.

Plan Your Shows:

- Request Hour: Play your favorite tracks by request.
- News Segment: Share the latest bunker updates or any news you can gather from the outside world.
- Storytelling Hour: Read aloud from a book or make up your own stories. You could even have a serialized adventure that continues each day.

Start Broadcasting:

- Announce your songs like a pro DJ. For example, "And now, folks, for our top hit of the day, here's a classic from the '80s to get you dancing in your bunker!"

Record and Replay Shows:

- If you have a way to record your broadcasts, do so. You can play them back later or share them with your bunker buddies who missed the live show.

Rotate DJs:

- Take turns being the DJ to give everyone a chance to host their own show. This keeps things fresh and exciting.

Keeping the Station Running

- Regular Schedule: Set a schedule for your radio shows. This gives everyone something to look forward to each day.
- Interactive Elements: Have call-ins or write-ins (you can use walkie-talkies or notes) for song requests and shout-outs.
- Special Segments: Introduce special segments like "Fun Fact of the Day," "Mystery Song Challenge," or "Bunker Trivia."

Radio Station Names

- Bunker Beats FM
- Underground Jams Radio
- Apocalypse Airwaves
- Survival Soundtrack Station
- Fallout FM
- Shelter Shuffles Radio
- Hidden Hits HQ
- Crisis Countdown Radio
- Quarantine Q-Radio
- Endtime Echoes
- Radio Resilience
- Disaster DJ Network
- Sanctuary Sounds
- Cavern Classics
- Vault Vibes Radio
- Echo Chamber FM

- Survival Symphony
- Bunker Boogie
- Rescue Radio
- Doomsday DJ Central

Chapter 1 Recap Quiz: Let's Check Your Learning!

Okay, let's see how much you've learned from Chapter 1! Here's a 15-question multiple-choice quiz to test your knowledge. Lets see how many you can get right!

1. Why is reinforced concrete recommended for bunker walls?

A. It's lightweight and easy to install
B. It absorbs radiation and withstands blasts
C. It's the cheapest material available
D. It keeps the bunker warm

2. What is the purpose of using activated carbon filters in a bunker ventilation system?

A. To add a pleasant scent
B. To filter out radioactive particles
C. To eliminate harmful gases
D. To reduce noise

3. What should you consider when choosing the location for your bunker?

A. Proximity to a shopping center
B. Concealment and easy access
C. Distance from your house
D. Availability of Wi-Fi

4. Which of these is a primary benefit of using deep cycle batteries in your bunker?

A. They are the cheapest batteries

B. They require no maintenance

C. They are designed for repeated charging and discharging

D. They are lightweight and portable

5. What is the role of HEPA filtration systems in a bunker?

A. To provide heat during winter

B. To filter out radioactive particles and contaminants

C. To cool the bunker in summer

D. To recycle water

6. Why is it crucial to have a manual crank ventilation system as a backup?

A. It's quieter than electric systems

B. It works without electricity

C. It's easier to install

D. It's more efficient

7. How should you arrange the interior space of your bunker for maximum efficiency?

A. Place all furniture in the center of the room

B. Use foldable and multi-functional furniture

C. Leave everything unpacked for flexibility

D. Install permanent structures everywhere

8. Which type of insulation is recommended for maintaining a stable temperature in your bunker?

A. Fiberglass insulation

B. Spray foam or rigid foam boards

C. Bubble wrap

D. Thin plastic sheets

9. How can you ensure a secure entrance and exit for your bunker?

A. Use heavy-duty, blast-resistant doors with locks

B. Use regular wooden doors with padlocks

C. Use sliding glass doors

D. Have only one hidden entrance

10. What's an essential step in managing waste in a bunker?

    A. Installing a high-tech waste incinerator

    B. Using a composting or chemical toilet

    C. Dumping waste outside periodically

    D. Storing waste in sealed plastic bags indefinitely

11. How much water should be stored in the bunker for a family of four for two weeks?

    A. 28 gallons

    B. 42 gallons

    C. 56 gallons

    D. 70 gallons

12. Which country is known for having extensive underground facilities built during the Cold War?

    A. Canada

    B. Russia

    C. Australia

    D. Brazil

13. Why might some modern bunkers include features like swimming pools and theaters?

    A. To attract tourists

    B. To enhance survival experience and morale

    C. To comply with new building regulations

    D. To increase property value

14. What's a key reason for using solar panels as a power source in a bunker?

    A. They are the cheapest option available

    B. They provide unlimited power without fuel

    C. They are easy to install underground

    D. They require no maintenance

15. What's an example of a creative bunker activity that can also serve a functional purpose?

    A. Decorating the bunker walls with graffiti
    B. Setting up a radio station to provide news and entertainment
    C. Building a swimming pool for exercise
    D. Installing a home theater for movie nights

> "A bunker is a place where you can survive, thrive, and keep your sanity when the world outside goes mad."
>
> "Preparedness is the key to survival, and your bunker is the ultimate tool in that arsenal."
>
> "In the face of adversity, our greatest weapon is our ability to adapt, and nothing exemplifies this more than a well-built bunker."

Answers

Why is reinforced concrete recommended for bunker walls?

    B. It absorbs radiation and withstands blasts

What is the purpose of using activated carbon filters in a bunker ventilation system?

    C. To eliminate harmful gases

What should you consider when choosing the location for your bunker?

    B. Concealment and easy access

Which of these is a primary benefit of using deep cycle batteries in your bunker?

    C. They are designed for repeated charging and discharging

What is the role of HEPA filtration systems in a bunker?

B. To filter out radioactive particles and contaminants

Why is it crucial to have a manual crank ventilation system as a backup?

B. It works without electricity

How should you arrange the interior space of your bunker for maximum efficiency?

B. Use foldable and multi-functional furniture

Which type of insulation is recommended for maintaining a stable temperature in your bunker?

B. Spray foam or rigid foam boards

How can you ensure a secure entrance and exit for your bunker?

A. Use heavy-duty, blast-resistant doors with locks

What's an essential step in managing waste in a bunker?

B. Using a composting or chemical toilet

How much water should be stored in the bunker for a family of four for two weeks?

C. 56 gallons

Which country is known for having extensive underground facilities built during the Cold War?

B. Russia

Why might some modern bunkers include features like swimming pools and theaters?

B. To enhance survival experience and morale

What's a key reason for using solar panels as a power source in a bunker?

B. They provide unlimited power without fuel

What's an example of a creative bunker activity that can also serve a functional purpose?

B. Setting up a radio station to provide news and entertainment

Did you know that the world's largest underground bunker complex is located in the Svalbard Archipelago, Norway?

The Svalbard Global Seed Vault, also known as the "Doomsday Vault," is an underground bunker designed to preserve a wide variety of plant seeds from around the world in the event of global catastrophes. Situated about 130 meters deep inside a mountain on the remote island of Spitsbergen, it is built to withstand natural and man-made disasters, including nuclear war and global warming. The facility can store up to 4.5 million seed samples, making it a crucial resource for biodiversity and food security in the future.

- By storing these seeds, the vault ensures that in the event of an agricultural crisis caused by natural disasters, climate change, disease outbreaks, or human-made catastrophes, the seeds can be used to restore agricultural systems and sustain food production.
- This genetic diversity is vital for developing resilient crop varieties that can adapt to changing environmental conditions and evolving pests and diseases, making the Svalbard Global Seed Vault a critical insurance policy for humanity's future.
- The Svalbard Global Seed Vault is designed to remain frozen even without power, thanks to the naturally cold permafrost surrounding it, ensuring that the seeds remain preserved for centuries even in the event of a power failure or extreme global warming scenarios.

Chapter 2: Nuclear Fallout

What Is Nuclear Fallout?

Nuclear fallout, also known simply as fallout, refers to the residual radioactive material propelled into the upper atmosphere following a nuclear explosion or a nuclear reactor incident. This material, composed of radioactive dust and ash, eventually falls back to Earth, contaminating the environment with harmful radiation. The intensity and duration of this fallout depend on the size of the explosion, the type of nuclear device used, and the prevailing weather conditions. Fallout can spread over vast areas, posing severe risks to human health and the environment.

"Nuclear fallout is the silent, unseen enemy that lingers long after the initial explosion, posing a persistent threat to all life forms."

The primary danger of nuclear fallout lies in its radioactive particles, which can be inhaled, ingested, or absorbed through the skin. These particles emit radiation that can cause acute radiation sickness, increase the risk of cancer, and lead to genetic mutations. The severity of these health effects depends on the level of exposure and the duration for which individuals are exposed. Immediate fallout, which occurs within the first 24 hours of a nuclear explosion, is especially dangerous, with high levels of radiation that can be lethal. Long-term fallout, while less intense, continues to pose health risks for years or even decades.

"In the event of a nuclear explosion, the real danger lies not just in the blast itself, but in the insidious fallout that follows, spreading radiation far and wide."

To mitigate the effects of nuclear fallout, people are advised to seek shelter in reinforced structures, ideally underground bunkers, that can block or reduce the penetration of radioactive particles. Stockpiling essential supplies such as food, water, and medical kits is crucial for long-term survival. Additionally, understanding and implementing decontamination procedures, such as removing contaminated clothing and washing exposed skin, can significantly reduce the risks associated with fallout. As awareness and preparedness are key, it is essential to educate oneself about the nature of nuclear fallout and the necessary steps to protect against its harmful effects.

"Preparedness against nuclear fallout involves not only immediate action but a long-term commitment to safety and decontamination."

How Radiation Works and How to Survive It

Radiation is energy that comes from a source and travels through space at the speed of light. It can be in the form of particles or electromagnetic waves. There are two main types of radiation: ionizing and non-ionizing.

1. Ionizing Radiation:

- Types: Includes alpha particles, beta particles, gamma rays, and X-rays.

- Danger: Ionizing radiation is harmful because it has enough energy to remove tightly bound electrons from atoms, creating ions. This process can damage or destroy cells and DNA, potentially leading to cancer and other health issues.

2. Non-Ionizing Radiation:

- Types: Includes ultraviolet (UV) light, visible light, infrared radiation, microwaves, and radio waves.

- Danger: Generally less harmful, but prolonged exposure to UV light can cause skin cancer, and high levels of microwave radiation can cause burns.

Sources of Radiation

Radiation can come from natural sources, such as the sun and radioactive materials in the earth, or from human-made sources, such as medical imaging equipment, nuclear power plants, and nuclear weapons.

1. Natural Sources:

- Cosmic radiation from space
- Radon gas from the earth
- Radioactive materials in the soil and rocks

2. Human-Made Sources:

- Medical imaging (X-rays, CT scans)
- Nuclear power plant emissions
- Fallout from nuclear weapons testing

How to Survive Radiation Exposure

Surviving radiation exposure involves understanding the principles of time, distance, and shielding. Here's how to apply these principles to protect yourself:

1. Time:

- Minimize Exposure: Limit the amount of time you spend exposed to radiation. The less time you are exposed, the lower your dose of radiation.

2. Distance:

- Increase Distance: The farther you are from the source of radiation, the lower your exposure. Radiation intensity decreases sharply with distance.

3. Shielding:

- Use Barriers: Use materials like lead, concrete, or even water to shield yourself from radiation. The thicker and denser the material, the better it can block or reduce radiation.

Practical Tips for Radiation Survival

1. Prepare a Radiation Emergency Kit:

- Include essentials like non-perishable food, water, a flashlight, batteries, a hand-crank radio, a first-aid kit, and potassium iodide tablets (to protect the thyroid from radioactive iodine).

2. Build a Safe Shelter:

- Basement or Inner Room: Create a fallout shelter in your basement or an interior room with no windows. These locations are more shielded from radiation.

- Thick Walls: Use thick materials like concrete or bricks to construct your shelter. If you're inside a building, stay in the center, away from exterior walls and roofs.

3. Stay Informed:

- Monitor News: Keep up-to-date with news from reliable sources. Use a battery-powered or hand-crank radio to listen to emergency broadcasts.

- Follow Instructions: Adhere to instructions from authorities regarding evacuation or sheltering in place.

4. Personal Protection:

- Wear Protective Clothing: If you must go outside, wear long sleeves, pants, and a hat to cover as much skin as possible. Use a mask or a cloth to cover your nose and mouth to avoid inhaling radioactive particles.

- Decontaminate: Remove contaminated clothing and wash your body thoroughly with soap and water if you think you've been exposed to radiation.

Potassium Iodide (KI) Tablets

Potassium iodide tablets can help protect your thyroid gland from radioactive iodine. The thyroid gland absorbs iodine from the bloodstream to produce hormones. By taking non-radioactive iodine in the form of KI tablets, you can prevent the thyroid from absorbing the harmful radioactive iodine. However, KI tablets do not protect against other types of radiation or radioactive materials.

1. When to Take KI Tablets:

- Take KI tablets only when instructed by public health or emergency response officials, usually after a nuclear event has released radioactive iodine into the environment.

2. Dosage:

- Follow the dosage instructions provided with the KI tablets. Dosages vary based on age and health condition.

Crazy Facts About Radiation

- Banana Equivalent Dose: Bananas are naturally radioactive due to their high potassium content. Eating one banana exposes you to about 0.1 microsieverts of radiation. This small amount is harmless, but the concept of the "Banana Equivalent Dose" is used to help people understand everyday radiation exposure.

- The Elephant's Foot: Deep inside the Chernobyl Nuclear Power Plant lies a highly radioactive mass known as the "Elephant's Foot." Made of melted reactor core material, it's so deadly that spending just 30 seconds near it can deliver a lethal dose of radiation.

- Space Radiation: Astronauts in space are exposed to higher levels of cosmic radiation. During a mission to Mars, astronauts could be exposed to the equivalent of 100 times the annual radiation dose experienced on Earth. This exposure increases the risk of cancer and other health issues.

- Glow-in-the-Dark Paint: During the early 20th century, glow-in-the-dark paint was made using radium. Workers, known as the "Radium Girls," would often lick their paint brushes to create fine points, unknowingly ingesting dangerous amounts of radium, leading to severe health problems.

- The Oklo Natural Reactor: Around 2 billion years ago, a natural nuclear reactor operated in Oklo, Gabon, Africa. Groundwater seeped into a uranium-rich deposit, triggering a sustained nuclear fission reaction. This natural reactor ran for hundreds of thousands of years, producing radiation and nuclear waste, much like a modern reactor.

- Fukushima's Radioactive Wild Boars: After the Fukushima Daiichi nuclear disaster in 2011, the evacuated area saw a rise in the population of wild boars. These boars have since been found to have high levels of radiation, making them dangerous to humans and other animals.

- Marie Curie's Notebook: Marie Curie, the pioneering scientist who discovered radioactivity, conducted many of her experiments with radium. Her notebooks, and even her cookbooks, are still so radioactive that they are stored in lead-lined boxes and can only be handled with protective gear.

- Thorium and Lantern Mantles: Lantern mantles used for camping often contain thorium, a radioactive element. When heated, thorium emits a bright light. While the amount of radiation is minimal, it's enough to be detected with a Geiger counter.

- The Most Radioactive Place on Earth: The most radioactive spot on Earth is in the basement of the Chernobyl Nuclear Power Plant, near the "Elephant's Foot." The radiation levels there are so high that it's impossible to stay near it for more than a few seconds without suffering severe health effects.
- Radiation and Evolution: Some scientists believe that low levels of natural radiation have played a role in the evolution of life on Earth. Natural background radiation can cause mutations in DNA, which over long periods, contribute to genetic diversity and evolution.

Safest Places During a Nuclear War

Imagine a scenario where tensions escalate to the brink of a nuclear war. Knowing where to seek refuge could be crucial for survival. Here are three of the safest places to be if such an unfortunate event were to occur. These countries are considered safe due to their geographical isolation, lack of involvement in global conflicts, and minimal nuclear targets.

1. New Zealand

New Zealand is often cited as one of the safest places during a nuclear war. Its remote location in the South Pacific, far from major nuclear powers and conflict zones, makes it an ideal refuge.

- Geographical Isolation: Far from any major nuclear powers, reducing the risk of direct attacks or fallout.
- Political Neutrality: Historically maintains a neutral stance in global conflicts, reducing the risk of being a target.
- Self-Sufficiency: Strong agricultural industry ensures food security, even in a global crisis.

2. Iceland

Iceland's remote location in the North Atlantic Ocean and its lack of military involvement make it a safe haven during a nuclear war.

- Remote Location: Far from major nuclear arsenals and political tensions.
- Low Population Density: Reduces the impact of any potential fallout.
- Geothermal Energy: Provides self-sufficient, sustainable energy, essential during global disruptions.

3. Switzerland

Switzerland is known for its neutrality and extensive civil defense infrastructure, including numerous fallout shelters built during the Cold War.

- Political Neutrality: Long-standing policy of neutrality keeps it out of international conflicts.
- Bunker Network: Extensive network of fallout shelters capable of housing the entire population.
- Mountainous Terrain: Natural barriers that could mitigate the impact of nuclear fallout.

Scenario: Escaping to Safety

Imagine you're in a country on the brink of nuclear conflict. The tension is palpable, and the threat of nuclear war is imminent. You need to decide quickly where to go to ensure your safety. With your family, you weigh your options and consider the safest places to relocate.

You first think of New Zealand. The idea of the picturesque landscapes and distant location from any nuclear power provides a sense of relief. You envision settling in a quiet, rural area, far from any major cities, living off the land, and enjoying the natural beauty while staying safe from global turmoil.

Next, Iceland comes to mind. The thought of its stunning, icy landscapes and geothermal resources offers a sense of security. You imagine living in a cozy, geothermal-heated home, far from any potential targets. The country's commitment to peace and sustainability makes it an attractive refuge.

Finally, Switzerland's robust civil defense infrastructure catches your attention. You picture your family safely tucked away in a well-equipped fallout shelter, surrounded by the beautiful Swiss Alps. The country's long standing neutrality and preparedness provide reassurance that you would be well-protected in the event of a nuclear war.

Countries with Nuclear Weapons

It's important to be aware of which countries possess nuclear weapons, as these nations are most likely to be involved in or targeted during a nuclear conflict. Here is a list of countries known to have nuclear arsenals:

- United States
- Russia
- China
- France
- United Kingdom
- India
- Pakistan
- North Korea
- Israel (undeclared but widely believed to possess nuclear weapons)

Given this information, choosing a safe place far from these nuclear powers is crucial for survival. The countries listed as the safest—New Zealand, Iceland, and Switzerland—provide a combination of geographical isolation, political neutrality, and robust infrastructure, making them ideal refuges during a nuclear war.

Building a Radiation-Proof Shelter

Building a radiation-proof shelter is essential for surviving a nuclear fallout. The primary goal is to create a space that can protect you from the harmful effects of radiation by blocking or reducing the penetration of radioactive particles. Start by selecting a location that offers maximum protection, such as a basement or an underground space. If you don't have access to an underground area, choose an interior room with no windows. The key to effective shielding is using materials that are dense and thick enough to absorb or deflect radiation. Concrete, lead, and steel are excellent choices, with concrete being the most practical and cost-effective for home construction. Your walls should be at least three feet thick, and you should reinforce them with steel rebar for added strength.

Once the structure is in place, focus on the interior to ensure it's fully equipped for long-term habitation. Install a ventilation system with HEPA and activated carbon filters to keep out radioactive particles and harmful gases. Ensure you have a reliable power source, such as a combination of solar panels and batteries, to maintain lighting, heating, and essential appliances. Stockpile non-perishable food, bottled water, and medical supplies, and create designated areas for sleeping, eating, and hygiene. Effective insulation is crucial for maintaining a stable temperature, so use materials like spray foam or rigid foam boards. Finally, implement decontamination procedures for anyone entering the shelter, such as removing outer clothing and washing exposed skin. With careful planning and construction, your radiation-proof shelter will be a safe haven during a nuclear fallout.

Crazy Facts

1. **Concrete Tunnels**: In Japan, there are secret concrete tunnels designed to withstand nuclear fallout, complete with emergency supplies and advanced filtration systems.
2. **Underground Luxury**: Some modern homes are being built with hidden underground bunkers that include luxury amenities like cinemas, spas, and gyms.

3. **Bunker Tours**: In some countries, you can take guided tours of historic Cold War-era bunkers, learning about their construction and the strategies behind their designs.
4. **Bunker Construction Kits**: In the U.S., companies offer DIY bunker construction kits that come with pre-fabricated materials and step-by-step instructions.
5. **Solar-Powered Bunkers**: Some advanced bunkers are equipped with solar panels and battery banks to ensure a renewable energy source during extended periods of isolation.
6. **Celebrity Bunkers**: Several Hollywood celebrities have invested in high-tech bunkers, complete with recording studios and private theaters.
7. **Water Purification Systems**: Cutting-edge water purification systems in some bunkers can turn contaminated water into safe drinking water, ensuring a sustainable water supply.
8. **Floating Shelters**: There are concepts for floating bunkers designed to survive nuclear fallout at sea, providing a mobile and isolated refuge.
9. **Geothermal Energy**: Some bunkers are built with geothermal heating systems, using the Earth's natural heat to maintain a comfortable temperature.
10. **Bio-Domes**: Future bunker designs include bio-domes with self-sustaining ecosystems, allowing inhabitants to grow their own food and recycle water.

History of Nuclear War Quiz

Who is considered the "father of the atomic bomb"?

A. Albert Einstein
B. Robert Oppenheimer
C. Enrico Fermi
D. Niels Bohr

What was the name of the project by the USA to develop the atomic bomb?

    A. The Apollo Project

    B. The Trinity Project

    C. The Manhattan Project

    D. The Mercury Project

Where was the first successful test of an atomic bomb conducted?

    A. Los Alamos, New Mexico

    B. Nevada Test Site, Nevada

    C. Trinity Site, New Mexico

    D. Oak Ridge, Tennessee

On what date was the atomic bomb dropped on Hiroshima?

    A. August 6, 1945

    B. August 9, 1945

    C. July 16, 1945

    D. September 2, 1945

What was the codename of the atomic bomb dropped on Hiroshima?

    A. Little Boy

    B. Fat Man

    C. Thin Man

    D. Tall Boy

Which city was the second to be hit by an atomic bomb?

    A. Tokyo

    B. Nagasaki

    C. Osaka

    D. Kyoto

What was the immediate death toll in Hiroshima following the atomic bomb explosion?

    A. 20,000

    B. 50,000

C. 80,000

D. 140,000

Which two countries were primarily involved in the Cold War?

A. United States and Germany

B. United States and Japan

C. United States and Soviet Union

D. United States and China

What was the main ideological conflict during the Cold War?

A. Democracy vs. Monarchy

B. Communism vs. Democracy

C. Fascism vs. Communism

D. Capitalism vs. Fascism

What was the name of the first artificial satellite launched by the Soviet Union, marking a significant event in the Cold War?

A. Apollo

B. Sputnik

C. Luna

D. Vostok

What event in 1962 brought the world to the brink of nuclear war?

A. The Berlin Airlift

B. The Cuban Missile Crisis

C. The Korean War

D. The Vietnam War

Which U.S. president played a crucial role during the Cuban Missile Crisis?

A. Dwight D. Eisenhower

B. John F. Kennedy

C. Richard Nixon

D. Lyndon B. Johnson

What was the primary purpose of the North Atlantic Treaty Organization (NATO) formed during the Cold War?

   A. To promote economic cooperation
   B. To provide collective defense against the Soviet Union
   C. To facilitate global trade
   D. To advance scientific research

What was the Strategic Defense Initiative (SDI), proposed by President Ronald Reagan?

   A. A plan to reduce nuclear arsenals
   B. A missile defense system to protect the United States from nuclear attack
   C. A space exploration program
   D. An economic aid package for Europe

When did the Cold War officially end?

   A. 1985
   B. 1989
   C. 1991
   D. 1995

"I am become Death, the destroyer of worlds." – Robert Oppenheimer

"The release of atomic energy has not created a new problem. It has merely made more urgent the necessity of solving an existing one." – Albert Einstein

"We knew the world would not be the same. A few people laughed, a few people cried. Most people were silent." – Robert Oppenheimer

Answers - History of Nuclear War

Who is considered the "father of the atomic bomb"?

Answer: B. Robert Oppenheimer

Robert Oppenheimer was a theoretical physicist who played a leading role in the Manhattan Project. He is famously quoted as saying, "Now I am become Death, the destroyer of worlds," from the Bhagavad Gita, after witnessing the first successful test of the atomic bomb.

What was the name of the project led by Robert Oppenheimer to develop the atomic bomb?

Answer: C. The Manhattan Project

The Manhattan Project was a secret research and development project during World War II that produced the first nuclear weapons. It was named after the Manhattan Engineer District of the U.S. Army Corps of Engineers.

Where was the first successful test of an atomic bomb conducted?

Answer: C. Trinity Site, New Mexico

The test, codenamed "Trinity," took place on July 16, 1945, in the Jornada del Muerto desert. The explosion was equivalent to 20,000 tons of TNT and marked the beginning of the nuclear age.

On what date was the atomic bomb dropped on Hiroshima?

Answer: A. August 6, 1945

The bomb dropped on Hiroshima was the first nuclear weapon used in warfare. The explosion killed an estimated 140,000 people by the end of 1945 due to the blast, heat, and radiation effects.

What was the codename of the atomic bomb dropped on Hiroshima?

Answer: A. Little Boy

"Little Boy" was a uranium-235 gun-type bomb. It was dropped by the B-29 bomber Enola Gay, piloted by Colonel Paul Tibbets.

Which city was the second to be hit by an atomic bomb?

Answer: B. Nagasaki

The bomb dropped on Nagasaki on August 9, 1945, was codenamed "Fat Man." It was a plutonium implosion-type bomb, similar to the one tested at the Trinity Site.

What was the immediate death toll in Hiroshima following the atomic bomb explosion?

Answer: C. 80,000

Approximately 80,000 people were killed instantly, with the total number of deaths rising to around 140,000 by the end of the year due to radiation injuries and other aftermath effects.

Which two countries were primarily involved in the Cold War?

Answer: C. United States and Soviet Union

The Cold War was a period of geopolitical tension between the United States and the Soviet Union and their respective allies. It was marked by political, military, and economic conflicts but did not result in direct large-scale fighting between the two superpowers.

What was the main ideological conflict during the Cold War?

Answer: B. Communism vs. Democracy

The United States represented democratic capitalist ideologies, while the Soviet Union was the leading proponent of communism. This ideological divide led to various proxy wars and the arms race.

What was the name of the first artificial satellite launched by the Soviet Union, marking a significant event in the Cold War?

Answer: B. Sputnik

Launched on October 4, 1957, Sputnik 1 was the first artificial Earth satellite. Its launch marked the beginning of the space age and the U.S.-Soviet space race.

What event in 1962 brought the world to the brink of nuclear war?

Answer: B. The Cuban Missile Crisis

The Cuban Missile Crisis occurred in October 1962 when the United States discovered Soviet ballistic missiles in Cuba. The crisis was resolved when the Soviet Union agreed to dismantle the missiles in exchange for the U.S. promising not to invade Cuba and secretly removing U.S. missiles from Turkey.

Which U.S. president played a crucial role during the Cuban Missile Crisis?

Answer: B. John F. Kennedy

President Kennedy's administration negotiated with Soviet Premier Nikita Khrushchev to de-escalate the crisis. Kennedy's leadership during the crisis is often praised for averting a potential nuclear war.

What was the primary purpose of the North Atlantic Treaty Organization (NATO) formed during the Cold War?

Answer: B. To provide collective defense against the Soviet Union

NATO was established in 1949 as a military alliance of Western countries. Its purpose was to provide mutual defense against the threat posed by the Soviet Union and its allies.

What was the Strategic Defense Initiative (SDI), proposed by President Ronald Reagan?

Answer: B. A missile defense system to protect the United States from nuclear attack

Announced in 1983, SDI, commonly known as "Star Wars," aimed to develop a space-based missile defense system that could intercept and destroy incoming ballistic missiles. The initiative was never fully developed but significantly influenced U.S.-Soviet relations.

When did the Cold War officially end?

Answer: C. 1991

The Cold War ended with the dissolution of the Soviet Union in December 1991, leading to the emergence of the United States as the world's sole superpower and significant geopolitical changes.

Chapter 3: Zombie Outbreak

"When life gives you zombies, build a treehouse and make friends with the living."

It's an ordinary day in your bustling city when suddenly, chaos erupts. Distant screams echo through the streets, and you see people running frantically. The unimaginable has happened—a zombie apocalypse is upon you. As the living dead begin to roam the city, your primary thought is survival. With a mix of fear and determination, you and your friends decide to band together, transforming your once mundane routine into a critical fight for survival.

Your group quickly finds refuge in an abandoned building, barricading the doors with anything you can find. The eerie silence is occasionally broken by the moans of wandering zombies outside. You and your friends understand that staying in one place isn't a long-term solution. You need to fortify your hideout, gather supplies, and develop a plan to ensure your safety. The idea of building a zombie-proof treehouse excites you—it's the ultimate childhood dream turned into a survival necessity.

"Brains are overrated. Keep yours intact and outsmart the undead!"

Days are spent scavenging for food and supplies. You master the art of dumpster diving, uncovering hidden treasures that others have overlooked. Every outing becomes an adventure, filled with the thrill of evading zombies and the satisfaction of finding essential resources. You even start crafting DIY weapons, from slingshots to makeshift spears, turning everyday items into tools of survival.

"Surviving a zombie apocalypse is 90% preparation, 10% epic escape plans."

Understanding Zombies: Fact vs. Fiction

Zombies have long been a staple of horror fiction, captivating imaginations with their eerie, mindless hunger for human flesh. However, separating fact from fiction is crucial when preparing for any potential threat. Let's delve into the myths and realities surrounding zombies.

Fiction: The Traditional Zombie

In popular culture, zombies are often depicted as reanimated corpses, brought back to life through supernatural means or a viral infection. They are usually portrayed as slow-moving, decaying beings with a single-minded drive to consume the living. This portrayal is largely derived from folklore, particularly Haitian Vodou traditions, and has been popularized by countless books, movies, and television shows.

- **Supernatural Origins**: In many stories, zombies are created through magical rituals or curses. This supernatural element is purely fictional and has no basis in scientific reality.
- **Viral Infections**: More modern interpretations involve a viral outbreak that turns people into zombies. Movies like "28 Days Later" and "World War Z" depict fast-moving, rabid zombies resulting from a contagious disease.
- **Decaying Appearance**: Fictional zombies are often shown with rotting flesh, missing limbs, and other grotesque features, adding to their horror.

Fact: Real-World Parallels

While real zombies as depicted in fiction do not exist, there are phenomena in nature and medicine that resemble certain aspects of zombie lore.

- **Parasites and Fungi**: Some parasites and fungi can control the behavior of their hosts in ways that resemble "zombie-like" behavior. For example, the Ophiocordyceps fungus infects ants, taking over their nervous systems and forcing them to climb to a high point before killing them and releasing spores. This is often referred to as the "zombie-ant fungus."
- **Rabies**: Rabies is a viral disease that affects the central nervous system, causing aggressive behavior and increased saliva production. While not creating zombies, it provides a real-world example of how a virus can drastically alter behavior.
- **Neurotoxins**: Certain toxins can induce a state of paralysis or near-death, leading to mistaken declarations of death. In Haitian culture, the use of tetrodotoxin (found in pufferfish) has been linked to "zombification," where individuals appear dead and are later revived in a disoriented state.

Fiction: Zombie Apocalypse Scenarios

Stories often feature a complete societal collapse due to a zombie outbreak, with small groups of survivors fighting for their lives. These scenarios create dramatic and suspenseful narratives but are highly unlikely in reality.

- **Mass Infection**: Fictional outbreaks spread rapidly, infecting large populations within days or weeks. Real infectious diseases, even highly contagious ones, have more complex transmission dynamics and are often containable with modern medical interventions.
- **Survival Skills**: While learning survival skills is beneficial, the exaggerated dangers in zombie fiction can create unrealistic expectations about real-world emergencies.

Fact: Practical Preparedness

Despite the fictional nature of zombies, preparing for a zombie apocalypse can serve as a useful metaphor for general emergency preparedness. The skills and strategies often depicted—such as securing shelter, stockpiling supplies, and maintaining self-defense—are applicable to many disaster scenarios.

- **Emergency Kits**: Having a well-stocked emergency kit with food, water, medical supplies, and tools is essential for any disaster situation.
- **Community Planning**: Engaging with local emergency response plans and knowing evacuation routes can save lives during natural disasters, pandemics, or other emergencies.
- **Self-Defense**: Learning basic self-defense and first aid can increase your resilience and ability to protect yourself and others.

Why a Perimeter Alarm is needed?

When you're surviving a zombie apocalypse or camping in the wilderness, safety is a top priority. A perimeter alarm can serve as an early warning system against potential threats such as zombies, wild animals, or intruders. It allows you to sleep more soundly and focus on other survival tasks, knowing you'll be alerted to any danger approaching your camp.

Perimeter alarms are particularly useful in environments where visibility is limited, such as dense forests, or at night when you're most vulnerable. They can prevent surprise encounters with wildlife, deter curious animals or zombies from rummaging through your supplies, and give you crucial moments to prepare and react if an intruder approaches. This added layer of security can be the difference between a peaceful night and a stressful, dangerous situation. "Stay alert, stay safe—your perimeter alarm is the silent sentinel watching over your camp."

How to Set Up a Perimeter Alarm

Step 1: Choose Your Alarm Type

There are several types of perimeter alarms you can set up, depending on the materials available and the environment you're in. Some options include:

- Noise-Making Alarms: Simple and effective, these alarms use items like tin cans, pots, or bells strung together. When disturbed, they create noise to alert you.
- Tripwire Alarms: More sophisticated, these alarms use a tripwire connected to a noise-making device or a light source.
- Electronic Alarms: If you have access to electronic devices, motion sensors or portable alarms can be very effective.

Step 2: Identify Perimeter Points

Determine the most likely entry points around your campsite. These are the areas where an intruder or animal is most likely to approach. Focus on paths, open areas, and spots near food storage or water sources.

Step 3: Set Up the Alarm

For Noise-Making Alarms:

- Gather a collection of noisy items like tin cans, metal pots, or bells.
- String them together with a durable string or fishing line.
- Hang the string around your campsite at a height that would catch a passing animal or intruder.

For Tripwire Alarms:

- Find a length of thin, strong wire or cord.

- Attach one end of the tripwire to a stationary object (like a tree) at knee-height.
- Attach the other end to your noise-making device, such as a bell or tin can.
- Make sure the tripwire is taut and positioned so it will be disturbed by movement.

For Electronic Alarms:

- Place motion sensors around your campsite at strategic points.
- Set up the alarm device according to the manufacturer's instructions, ensuring it's activated and within range to detect movement.

Step 4: Test Your Alarm System

Before nightfall, test your alarm system to ensure it works correctly. Walk around the perimeter to see if the alarms are triggered as expected. Adjust the height and tension of tripwires or the position of noise-making items as needed.

Step 5: Monitor and Maintain

Regularly check your perimeter alarms to ensure they remain functional and haven't been disturbed by wind or weather. Replace or repair any parts that are damaged. Always stay vigilant and be prepared to respond quickly if your alarm is triggered.

"In the wilderness, a good night's sleep starts with a well-set perimeter alarm."

Makeshift Weapons

In the event of a zombie apocalypse, having weapons to defend yourself is crucial for survival. When traditional weapons aren't available, you'll need to get creative and use everyday items to protect yourself. Makeshift weapons can be fashioned from materials found in your surroundings, turning ordinary objects into life-saving tools.

The Solution: Improvise, Adapt, Overcome

Creating makeshift weapons involves utilizing common items and modifying them for defense. Here's how to arm yourself effectively:

Step 1: Identify Potential Weapons

Look around your immediate environment for items that can be repurposed as weapons. Consider the following:

- Blunt Objects: Baseball bats, hammers, heavy branches, or metal pipes can deliver powerful blows to a zombie's head.
- Sharp Objects: Kitchen knives, broken glass, shards of metal, or even a pair of scissors can be used for close combat.
- Improvised Spears: Long poles, broom handles, or sturdy branches with sharpened ends can keep zombies at a distance while inflicting damage.
- Flamethrowers: Hairspray or aerosol cans combined with a lighter can create a makeshift flamethrower to fend off zombies.
- Projectile Weapons: Slingshots, rocks, or even homemade bows and arrows can help you strike from a distance.

Step 2: Enhance Your Weapons

Modify and improve the found items to make them more effective:

- Blunt Objects: Wrap handles with cloth or tape to improve grip and prevent slipping during use.
- Sharp Objects: Sharpen the edges of metal scraps or broken glass carefully. Secure these sharp items to handles or poles to extend your reach.
- Improvised Spears: Secure a sharp object to the end of a pole using strong tape, rope, or wire to create a sturdy spear.

- Flamethrowers: Ensure you have a reliable ignition source and practice using the aerosol can and lighter safely to avoid accidents.
- Projectile Weapons: Fashion slingshots from sturdy branches and elastic bands. Use flexible branches for bows and create arrows from straight sticks with sharp tips.

Step 3: Practice and Prepare

Knowing how to use your makeshift weapons is as important as having them. Practice using them safely and effectively:

- Swinging Blunt Objects: Focus on aim and control, ensuring you can deliver powerful strikes without losing balance.
- Using Sharp Objects: Practice safe handling and precise strikes to vital points, such as the head or neck.
- Wielding Improvised Spears: Learn to thrust and withdraw quickly to keep zombies at bay.
- Operating Flamethrowers: Use in short bursts to conserve fuel and maximize impact. Aim for the zombies' heads to cause maximum damage.
- Shooting Projectile Weapons: Practice your aim and distance with slingshots or bows to ensure accuracy when it matters most.

Step 4: Stay Safe

While makeshift weapons can be effective, always prioritize your safety:

- Maintain Distance: Whenever possible, use weapons that allow you to keep a safe distance from zombies.
- Stay Aware: Be mindful of your surroundings and have an escape plan in case your weapon fails or more zombies approach.
- Work as a Team: If you're with others, coordinate your defense strategies to cover each other and improve your chances of survival.

"Brains are overrated. Keep yours intact and outsmart the undead!"

The Fun Fact: Did You Know?

Did you know that some of the most iconic weapons in zombie fiction, like the spiked baseball bat, originated from improvised ideas? These weapons highlight human ingenuity and the ability to adapt everyday items into tools for survival.

By creating makeshift weapons, you can enhance your defenses and improve your chances of surviving a zombie apocalypse. Remember, the key is to be resourceful, stay calm, and use your environment to your advantage.

Humans vs. Zombies: The Real Threat

Why Humans Can Be More Dangerous Than Zombies

In a zombie apocalypse, zombies are often portrayed as the primary threat. They are relentless, hungry, and numerous. However, in many scenarios, humans can pose a greater danger than the undead. Here's why:

1. Rational Thought and Unpredictability:

- Unlike zombies, which operate on basic instincts and predictable behavior, humans can think, plan, and adapt. This makes their actions far less predictable and potentially more dangerous. Humans can deceive, strategize, and manipulate situations to their advantage, posing a complex threat.

2. Desperation and Fear:

- In the chaotic world of a zombie apocalypse, fear and desperation can drive people to make irrational and dangerous decisions. The instinct to survive at all costs can lead to betrayal, violence, and ruthless behavior. Desperate people might fight over resources, steal, or even kill to ensure their own survival.

3. Competition for Resources:

- As supplies dwindle, the competition for food, water, shelter, and weapons becomes fierce. Unlike zombies, humans need these resources to survive and will go to great lengths to secure them. This competition can lead to conflicts, ambushes, and raids, making human encounters potentially deadly.

4. Breakdown of Social Order:

- The collapse of societal structures and law enforcement means there are no repercussions for criminal behavior. This lawlessness can result in an increase in looting, violence, and territorial disputes. Groups or individuals may form gangs or factions, enforcing their own rules and engaging in power struggles.

5. Emotional Reactions:

- Humans are driven by emotions, which can cloud judgment and lead to dangerous decisions. Anger, grief, jealousy, and panic can cause people to act recklessly, endangering themselves and others. Unlike zombies, humans can bear grudges, seek revenge, and let their emotions dictate their actions.

"Surviving a zombie apocalypse is 90% preparation, 10% epic escape plans."

How to Navigate Human Threats

1. Build Trust Carefully:

- Form alliances with caution. Trustworthy companions are invaluable, but be wary of those who may turn on you when resources are scarce.

2. Establish Clear Communication:

- Clear communication and established protocols can help prevent misunderstandings and conflicts within your group. Regularly check in with your companions and ensure everyone is on the same page.

3. Secure Resources Discreetly:

- Avoid drawing attention to your supplies. Store food, water, and other essentials in hidden locations. Sharing too much information about your resources can make you a target.

4. Stay Vigilant:

- Always be aware of your surroundings and the people in your vicinity. Set up perimeter alarms and keep watches at night to prevent ambushes.

5. Develop Conflict Resolution Skills:

- Learn to defuse tensions and resolve conflicts within your group. Keeping morale high and maintaining a cooperative environment can prevent internal disputes from escalating.

6. Prepare for Self-Defense:

- Be ready to defend yourself not just against zombies, but against potential human threats. This includes learning self-defense techniques, securing your living area, and having contingency plans.

"Brains are overrated. Keep yours intact and outsmart the undead-and the living!"

The Fun Fact: Did You Know?

Did you know that in many zombie movies and TV shows, the most significant danger often comes from other humans rather than zombies? Films like "The Walking Dead" and "28 Days Later" explore the theme of human conflict and the moral dilemmas faced in a lawless, post-apocalyptic world.

By understanding the potential threat posed by other humans, you can better prepare and strategize for a zombie apocalypse. Trust cautiously, secure resources, and always be ready to defend yourself from both the undead and the living.

Basic Self-Defense Techniques

Why Self-Defense is Crucial

In a zombie apocalypse, knowing how to defend yourself is not just a skill but a necessity. While zombies are a significant threat, human encounters can be equally dangerous. Learning basic self-defense techniques can give you the confidence and ability to protect yourself in various situations. Whether you're facing a physical attack from a desperate survivor or trying to fend off a zombie, self-defense can be the difference between life and death.

1. Situational Awareness:

- The first step in self-defense is being aware of your surroundings. Pay attention to potential threats and escape routes. Always have a plan for where you would go and what you would do if you were suddenly attacked. This heightened awareness can prevent many dangerous situations from escalating.

2. Defensive Stance and Movement:

- A proper stance is crucial for effective self-defense. Stand with your feet shoulder-width apart, knees slightly bent, and hands up to protect your face. This stance allows for better balance and readiness to react. Practice moving in this stance to maintain stability while dodging or countering attacks.

3. Blocking and Parrying:

- Learn how to block incoming attacks to protect vital areas like your head and torso. Use your forearms to deflect punches and kicks. Parrying, or redirecting the force of an attack, can also give you an opening to counter-attack or escape.

4. Striking Techniques:

- Knowing how to strike effectively is key to self-defense. Focus on vulnerable areas such as the eyes, nose, throat, and groin. Simple strikes like punches, elbows, and knee strikes can be very effective. Practice using your body's weight and momentum to increase the power of your strikes.

5. Escaping Holds and Grabs:

- Learn techniques to escape common holds and grabs. For example, if someone grabs your wrist, rotate your arm to break free or use leverage to reverse the hold. Understanding how to leverage your body's mechanics against an attacker's grip can help you quickly regain control.

6. Using Everyday Objects as Weapons:

- In a pinch, almost any object can become a defensive tool. Pens, keys, or even a flashlight can be used to strike an attacker. Larger items like chairs or sticks can be used to create distance and protect yourself. Practice thinking creatively about how to use your environment to your advantage.

7. Ground Defense:

- If you're knocked to the ground, knowing how to defend yourself is essential. Practice techniques for getting up quickly and safely while maintaining a defensive position. If you can't get up immediately, use your legs to kick and create distance from your attacker.

8. Psychological Tactics:

- Sometimes, self-defense is as much about psychology as it is about physical techniques. Shouting loudly can startle an attacker and attract attention. Displaying confidence, even if you don't feel it, can also deter potential threats. Use verbal de-escalation tactics to defuse situations whenever possible.

9. Training and Practice:

- Regular practice is crucial for effective self-defense. Consider joining a self-defense class or practicing with a partner. Drills and scenarios can help you respond more instinctively in real-life situations. The more you train, the more prepared you'll be to protect yourself and others.

The Fun Fact: Did You Know?

Did you know that martial arts like Krav Maga, which was developed for the Israeli Defense Forces, focus specifically on practical self-defense techniques? These systems teach you how to defend against multiple attackers and disarm opponents, making them particularly useful in unpredictable situations.

By mastering these basic self-defense techniques, you equip yourself with the tools to handle a variety of dangerous scenarios. Remember, the goal of self-defense is not just to fight back, but to survive and protect yourself effectively. Stay aware, stay prepared, and you can navigate the challenges of a zombie apocalypse—or any other threat—with greater confidence and security.

Crazy Facts

Adrenaline Boost: During a life-threatening situation, your body releases adrenaline, which can temporarily increase your strength and pain tolerance. This "fight or flight" response can be crucial in self-defense scenarios.

Animal Techniques: Some martial arts techniques are inspired by animal movements. For example, Kung Fu styles mimic the fighting strategies of animals like tigers, cranes, and snakes.

Pressure Points: There are specific pressure points on the human body that, when struck, can cause significant pain or even temporary paralysis. Martial artists often train to target these areas effectively.

Historical Weapons: Everyday items were often used as weapons in history. For instance, in feudal Japan, farmers used sickles and staffs for self-defense, which later evolved into martial arts weapons like the nunchaku.

Military Training: Modern military forces often incorporate martial arts into their training. For example, the U.S. Marine Corps uses a program called MCMAP (Marine Corps Martial Arts Program) that combines various fighting techniques.

Fast Reflexes: With consistent training, your reflexes can become so sharp that you can react to an attack in milliseconds. Professional fighters often have reaction times faster than the blink of an eye.

Voice as a Weapon: Shouting can be a powerful self-defense tool. Not only can it startle an attacker, but it also draws attention to your situation, potentially bringing help.

Breaking Boards: Martial artists often break wooden boards or bricks to demonstrate their striking power. This practice also helps them focus their strength and technique.

Unusual Training Methods: Some martial arts schools use unconventional training methods. For example, Shaolin monks are known to train by standing on one leg for hours or meditating under cold waterfalls to build endurance and mental toughness.

Evasion Techniques: Self-defense isn't just about fighting back. Techniques like rolling, dodging, and even running can be just as important in avoiding harm and escaping dangerous situations.

The Art of Camouflage: How to Hide in Plain Sight

Why Camouflage is Essential

In a zombie apocalypse, blending in with your surroundings can be a critical survival skill. While traditional camouflage techniques involve mimicking natural environments, hiding in plain sight during a zombie apocalypse might require a more unconventional approach: looking like a zombie. This strategy can help you move through dangerous areas undetected, avoid confrontations, and gather supplies safely.

How to Look Like a Zombie

Step 1: Study Zombie Behavior

To effectively mimic a zombie, you need to understand their behavior. Watch how they move and react. Typically, zombies have slow, unsteady gaits, vacant stares, and make guttural noises. Observing these traits will help you replicate them convincingly.

Step 2: Dress the Part

Your appearance should match that of a typical zombie. Here's how to achieve the look:

- Clothing: Wear old, tattered clothes that you don't mind dirtying or tearing. Zombies often appear disheveled, with ripped fabric and stains. Add some fake blood or dirt to your clothes for a more authentic look.
- Makeup: Use face paint or makeup to create a pale, gaunt appearance. Darken the areas around your eyes and add some fake blood around your mouth and on your clothes. You can use mud or charcoal to give your skin a dirty, decayed look.

Step 3: Master the Zombie Walk

Zombies are known for their distinctive, shambling walk. Practice moving with a slow, uneven gait. Let your arms hang loosely and drag your feet slightly. The goal is to look uncoordinated and sluggish. Try to keep your movements jerky and unpredictable.

Step 4: Perfect the Zombie Sound

While zombies don't speak, they do make noises. Practice low, guttural moans and groans. Avoid making human-like sounds such as talking or shouting. The more authentic your zombie sounds, the less likely you are to draw unwanted attention.

Step 5: Maintain a Vacant Expression

A key part of looking like a zombie is maintaining a blank, unfocused stare. Avoid eye contact with other humans, as this can give you away. Instead, look through people rather than at them, and keep your facial muscles relaxed.

Step 6: Move with the Horde

When near zombies, move in sync with their group. Mimic their pace and stay in the middle or at the edges of the horde to blend in. Avoid sudden movements that might make you stand out. If a zombie notices you, react slowly and without alarm to avoid drawing attention.

Step 7: Use Scents

Zombies are often depicted as being attracted to the scent of living humans. Mask your scent by using dirt, mud, or even zombie guts (if you're feeling particularly brave). This can help cover up your human smell and make your disguise more convincing.

Did You Know?

- Animal Camouflage Masters: Did you know that some animals, like the octopus, are masters of camouflage, able to change their color and texture to blend into their surroundings? These natural abilities allow them to hide from predators and sneak up on prey.

- Chameleon Color Change: Chameleons can change their skin color to communicate with other chameleons or to regulate their body temperature, in addition to blending into their environment. This makes them one of the most versatile camouflagers in the animal kingdom.
- Arctic Adaptations: Arctic animals like the snowshoe hare and Arctic fox change their fur color with the seasons, turning white in winter to blend in with the snow and brown in summer to match the tundra. This seasonal camouflage helps them avoid predators year-round.
- Leaf Mimicry: The leaf-tailed gecko of Madagascar has a tail that looks remarkably like a leaf, complete with veins and notches. This incredible mimicry helps it avoid detection by predators and prey alike.
- Human Camouflage Techniques: Military forces have long used camouflage to blend into various environments. Soldiers use face paint, ghillie suits, and patterned uniforms to break up their outline and blend into their surroundings during combat operations.
- Zombie Camouflage: While you can't change your skin like an octopus, you can use these principles to hide in plain sight during a zombie apocalypse. By mastering the art of looking like a zombie—through makeup, clothing, and behavior—you can move through dangerous areas more safely and gather supplies without drawing attention. The key to effective camouflage is observation and practice. The more convincingly you can mimic a zombie, the better your chances of surviving undetected in a world overrun by the undead.

How to Hide from Zombies

In a zombie apocalypse, staying hidden can be as crucial as being armed. Effective concealment can mean the difference between life and death. Here's how to master the art of hiding from zombies.

1. Choose the Right Hiding Spot

Selecting a good hiding spot is the first step in staying safe from zombies. Look for locations that provide both cover and concealment. Ideal spots include:

- **Elevated Areas**: Zombies have difficulty climbing. Seek refuge in treehouses, rooftops, or upper floors of buildings.
- **Enclosed Spaces**: Small, secure rooms with sturdy doors and minimal windows can keep zombies out.
- **Natural Cover**: Dense vegetation, thick bushes, and rocky areas can obscure you from view.

2. Use Natural and Man-Made Camouflage

Blend into your surroundings using natural and artificial camouflage. Here's how:

- **Natural Elements**: Cover yourself with mud, leaves, and other natural materials to break up your outline and reduce your scent.
- **Clothing**: Wear muted, earth-toned clothing that matches the environment. Avoid bright colors and reflective materials.
- **Camouflage Gear**: Use military-style camo netting and ghillie suits if available. These are designed to blend seamlessly with various terrains.

3. Stay Silent and Still

Zombies are often attracted to noise and movement. To avoid detection:

- **Move Quietly**: Walk softly, avoiding dry leaves, sticks, and noisy debris. Practice moving slowly and deliberately.

- **Hold Your Breath**: When zombies are near, remain as still and silent as possible. Even breathing can give you away.
- **Minimize Sounds**: Avoid talking, and be cautious with equipment that may produce noise, such as zippers or velcro.

4. Utilize Darkness and Shadows

Nighttime and shadowed areas can provide excellent cover from zombies.

- **Stay in the Shadows**: Move through shadowed areas whenever possible. Shadows obscure your form and make you harder to detect.
- **Use Nighttime to Your Advantage**: Zombies may have reduced vision in the dark. Use the cover of night to move or hide.
- **Avoid Using Lights**: Flashlights and fires can attract zombies. Use light sources sparingly and only when absolutely necessary.

5. Create Distractions

If you need to draw zombies away from your location or create an opportunity to escape:

- **Throw Objects**: Toss rocks or other objects to create noise away from your position. This can divert zombies' attention.
- **Set Up Decoys**: Set up noise-making devices like wind chimes or cans with pebbles to draw zombies to a different area.
- **Use Flares or Fireworks**: If you have access to flares or fireworks, use them strategically to lure zombies away.

6. Learn to Blend In

Mimicking zombie behavior can help you move through infested areas undetected.

- **Zombie Walk**: Practice a slow, shuffling walk with limp limbs. Avoid making sudden movements.

- **Zombie Sounds**: Imitate zombie moans and groans. This can help you blend in with a horde.
- **Zombie Scent**: Mask your scent with dirt or zombie guts to confuse zombies that rely on smell.

7. Monitor and Adapt

Always be ready to adapt your hiding strategy based on the situation:

- **Scout Ahead**: Before moving to a new hiding spot, scout the area for potential threats and escape routes.
- **Stay Alert**: Remain vigilant and ready to move if your hiding spot is compromised.
- **Change Locations**: If you're hiding long-term, periodically change locations to avoid being discovered by roaming zombies or other survivors.

Fun Facts

1. **Animal Mimicry**: Some animals, like the mimic octopus, can change their shape and behavior to imitate other animals as a defense mechanism. This is a perfect example of how mimicry can be used for survival.
2. **Camouflage History**: Camouflage has been used in military operations for over a century, evolving from simple earth-tone uniforms to complex digital patterns designed to blend in with various environments.
3. **Human Sense of Smell**: Humans have a surprisingly strong sense of smell. In survival situations, recognizing the scent of decay can help you detect nearby zombies before you see them.
4. **Zombie Hypnosis**: Some insects, like the emerald cockroach wasp, can effectively turn their prey into "zombies" by injecting them with a venom that controls their behavior. This is nature's version of zombification.

5. **Stealth Techniques**: Native American tribes used stealth techniques such as walking toe-to-heel to move quietly through the forest, a practice that can be adapted for avoiding zombies.
6. **Sound Distraction**: In World War II, soldiers used "sound ranging" to detect enemy positions based on noise. Similarly, creating sounds to distract zombies can be a key survival tactic.
7. **Night Vision**: While humans don't have natural night vision, training your eyes to adapt to darkness and using minimal light can improve your nighttime stealth.
8. **Scent Masking**: Hunters often use scent blockers to mask their presence from prey. Similar techniques can help you avoid detection by zombies.
9. **Predator Evasion**: Animals like deer and rabbits use zig-zag running patterns to evade predators. This tactic can be useful for escaping zombies.
10. **Urban Hideouts**: Many urban explorers use abandoned buildings and tunnels for exploration, skills that can be invaluable for finding hiding spots in a zombie-infested city.

Famous Zombies in Movies and TV Shows

1. Night of the Living Dead (1968)

"Night of the Living Dead," directed by George A. Romero, is often credited with popularizing the modern concept of zombies. The film follows a group of strangers who take refuge in a farmhouse to escape a horde of undead. These zombies are slow-moving, reanimated corpses that hunger for human flesh. The movie is notable for its social commentary, particularly on race and human nature, and it set the standard for many zombie tropes that followed.

- Slow-moving, relentless zombies
- Zombies created by unexplained causes
- The theme of humans turning on each other in crisis
- Use of a secluded farmhouse as a refuge
- Social commentary on race and society

"They're coming to get you, Barbara!"

2. The Walking Dead (2010-Present)

"The Walking Dead," based on the comic book series by Robert Kirkman, portrays a post-apocalyptic world overrun by zombies, referred to as "walkers." The series follows a group of survivors led by former sheriff Rick Grimes. The show delves deeply into the psychological and moral challenges faced by the characters as they navigate a world where the living can be more dangerous than the dead.

- Walkers are slow and decaying, attracted to noise
- Human survival is often more dangerous than the zombies
- Strong focus on character development and moral dilemmas
- The concept of communities and rebuilding society
- Themes of loss, hope, and resilience

"We are the walking dead."

3. World War Z (2013)

"World War Z," directed by Marc Forster and based on the novel by Max Brooks, features fast-moving, highly aggressive zombies. The protagonist, Gerry Lane, a former UN investigator, travels the world trying to find the source of the outbreak and a way to stop it. The film is notable for its large-scale action sequences and its depiction of a global response to the zombie pandemic.

- Fast, aggressive zombies that move in swarms
- Focus on global impact and international response
- Use of science and investigation to find a solution
- High-intensity action scenes and large-scale destruction

- Depiction of societal collapse and military intervention

"Movement is life."

4. 28 Days Later (2002)

Directed by Danny Boyle, "28 Days Later" introduces zombies through a rage-inducing virus. The story begins with Jim, a bicycle courier, waking up from a coma to find London deserted and overrun by infected humans. These "zombies" are not reanimated corpses but living people transformed by the virus. The film is known for its fast-paced, highly aggressive infected and its exploration of societal breakdown.

- Fast, rage-fueled infected rather than traditional zombies
- Exploration of the impact of isolation and societal collapse
- Themes of survival, fear, and human nature
- Use of a virus as the cause of the outbreak
- The gritty, realistic depiction of post-apocalyptic London

"That was longer than a heartbeat."

5. Shaun of the Dead (2004)

"Shaun of the Dead," directed by Edgar Wright, is a comedic take on the zombie genre. The film follows Shaun and his best friend Ed as they try to survive a zombie apocalypse in their small British town. Balancing horror and humor, the film pays homage to classic zombie movies while offering a fresh, humorous perspective.

- Slow, traditional zombies in a humorous context
- Blending of comedy with horror elements
- Emphasis on ordinary people dealing with extraordinary situations
- Satirical take on modern life and relationships
- Homages to classic zombie films and tropes

"You've got red on you."

Chapter 3: Zombies Outbreak Recap Quiz

Let's see how well you've grasped the essentials of surviving a zombie outbreak! Answer the following multiple-choice questions to test your knowledge.

1. What is the primary reason for building a zombie-proof treehouse?

    A. It's fun and brings back childhood memories.

    B. It offers a safe, elevated refuge from zombies.

    C. It's easier to decorate than an abandoned building.

    D. It can be seen as a status symbol among survivors.

2. Which of the following best describes the zombies in "Night of the Living Dead"?

    A. Fast and intelligent

    B. Slow-moving and relentless

    C. Virus-induced and rabid

    D. Controlled by a parasite

3. In "The Walking Dead," what are zombies referred to as?

    A. The Infected

    B. The Dead

    C. Walkers

    D. Creepers

4. Why is it important to master the art of dumpster diving during a zombie apocalypse?

    A. It's a form of entertainment.

    B. It helps in scavenging for essential supplies.

    C. It teaches you to be resourceful.

    D. It keeps you physically fit.

5. What is a key feature of the zombies depicted in "World War Z"?

    A. They are slow and decaying.

    B. They are fast and highly aggressive.

    C. They are created by a fungus.

    D. They are controlled by magic.

6. Which method is suggested for masking your scent from zombies?

    A. Wearing perfume

    B. Using zombie guts

    C. Applying insect repellent

    D. Spraying air freshener

7. What does situational awareness involve in the context of self-defense?

    A. Ignoring potential threats to stay calm

    B. Being aware of your surroundings and potential escape routes

    C. Practicing daily yoga to stay alert

    D. Constantly moving to avoid detection

8. In "28 Days Later," what is the cause of the zombie-like infection?

    A. A nuclear explosion

    B. A rage-inducing virus

    C. A parasitic fungus

    D. A voodoo curse

9. What is a recommended action when setting up a perimeter alarm?

    A. Place it only near food supplies.

    B. Use bright lights to deter zombies.

    C. Identify likely entry points and set alarms there.

    D. Set the alarm close to where you sleep for easy access.

10. Why can humans be more dangerous than zombies in an apocalypse?

    A. They are harder to detect.

    B. They can think, plan, and adapt.

    C. They are faster and stronger.

    D. They are immune to all types of attacks.

11. Which quote is associated with the movie "Night of the Living Dead"?

    A. "Brains are overrated."

    B. "They're coming to get you, Barbara!"

    C. "Movement is life."

    D. "You've got red on you."

12. What should you do if you're knocked to the ground by an attacker?

    A. Stay still and wait for help.

    B. Use your legs to kick and create distance.

    C. Shout for assistance.

    D. Play dead and hope they leave.

13. What is a key element of blending in with a zombie horde?

    A. Wearing bright clothing

    B. Walking quickly and confidently

    C. Mimicking zombie behavior and appearance

    D. Carrying a weapon openly

14. In "Shaun of the Dead," what is a significant theme?

    A. The effectiveness of military interventions

    B. The blending of comedy with horror

    C. The consequences of scientific experiments

    D. The use of advanced technology to survive

15. What type of alarm can be used in a campsite to detect approaching zombies or intruders?

    A. Bright lights

B. Noise-making alarms
C. Air horns
D. Motion-activated sprinklers

Chapter 3: Zombies Outbreak Recap Quiz Answers

What is the primary reason for building a zombie-proof treehouse?

B. It offers a safe, elevated refuge from zombies.

Which of the following best describes the zombies in "Night of the Living Dead"?

B. Slow-moving and relentless

In "The Walking Dead," what are zombies referred to as?

C. Walkers

Why is it important to master the art of dumpster diving during a zombie apocalypse?

B. It helps in scavenging for essential supplies.

What is a key feature of the zombies depicted in "World War Z"?

B. They are fast and highly aggressive.

Which method is suggested for masking your scent from zombies?

B. Using zombie guts

What does situational awareness involve in the context of self-defense?

B. Being aware of your surroundings and potential escape routes

In "28 Days Later," what is the cause of the zombie-like infection?

B. A rage-inducing virus

What is a recommended action when setting up a perimeter alarm?

C. Identify likely entry points and set alarms there.

Why can humans be more dangerous than zombies in an apocalypse?

B. They can think, plan, and adapt.

Which quote is associated with the movie "Night of the Living Dead"?

B. "They're coming to get you, Barbara!"

What should you do if you're knocked to the ground by an attacker?

B. Use your legs to kick and create distance.

What is a key element of blending in with a zombie horde?

C. Mimicking zombie behavior and appearance

In "Shaun of the Dead," what is a significant theme?

B. The blending of comedy with horror

What type of alarm can be used in a campsite to detect approaching zombies or intruders?

B. Noise-making alarms

Chapter 4: Forming a Faction Group

Why Factions Are Important?

In the chaotic world of any apocalyptic scenario, the formation of factions can be a crucial element for survival. Factions are groups of individuals who band together based on common goals, values, or survival strategies. They provide a structured support system, enhancing the chances of survival for their members. Within a faction, individuals can share resources, skills, and knowledge, creating a more resilient community. This collective effort not only increases the likelihood of survival but also provides a sense of belonging and purpose, which is vital for mental health in such dire circumstances.

> "Alone we can do so little; together we can do so much." – Helen Keller

Factions help establish order in the midst of chaos. In a world where societal norms have collapsed, factions can create their own rules and systems of governance. This can include assigning roles and responsibilities, establishing laws, and enforcing discipline. Such organization can prevent anarchy and internal conflict, ensuring that everyone works towards the common good. With clear leadership and structured operations, factions can effectively manage their resources, defend against threats, and plan for the future.

Another critical aspect of factions is the division of labor. In a well-organized faction, individuals can specialize in different roles based on their skills and strengths. For example, some members might focus on scavenging for supplies, while others concentrate on fortifying defenses or providing medical care. This specialization allows for more efficient use of resources and expertise, ensuring that all essential tasks are covered. Additionally, it fosters a sense of purpose among members, as everyone has a specific role that contributes to the group's overall survival.

"The strength of the team is each individual member. The strength of each member is the team." – Phil Jackson

Factions also provide a platform for mutual protection and defense. In any apocalyptic scenario, threats can come from environmental hazards, resource scarcity, or other desperate humans. A well-coordinated faction can organize patrols, set up perimeter defenses, and develop strategies to counter potential attacks. By pooling their collective strength and resources, factions can create a safer environment for their members. This collective defense mechanism is crucial for ensuring the long-term survival of the group, allowing them to thrive even in the face of constant danger.

Crazy Facts About Factions in Apocalyptic Scenarios

1. Historical Precedent: During historical plagues, such as the Black Death, people often formed small communities or factions to survive, pooling resources and skills.
2. Strength in Numbers: Studies in animal behavior show that many species form groups to enhance survival rates, such as herds of mammals or schools of fish.
3. Psychological Resilience: Being part of a faction can significantly boost morale and mental health, reducing the likelihood of psychological breakdowns.
4. Resource Management: Factions often develop intricate systems for resource management, including rationing and communal sharing, to ensure long-term survival.

5. Specialized Roles: In some survival scenarios, factions have developed roles such as "scouts" for gathering information and "guardians" for defense.
6. Cultural Evolution: Factions can evolve unique cultures, languages, and customs over time, influenced by their specific survival strategies and environments.
7. Technological Innovation: Historical factions have been known to innovate rapidly in response to crises, such as the development of new tools or weapons.
8. Economic Systems: Some factions establish their own economies, using barter systems or even creating their own currencies.
9. Social Hierarchies: Factions often develop complex social hierarchies and leadership structures, which can be based on merit, strength, or resource control.
10. Legendary Leaders: Many historical and fictional factions are remembered for their charismatic and effective leaders, who often become legendary figures in their own right.

By understanding the importance of factions and the dynamics within them, individuals can better prepare for survival in any end-of-the-world scenario. The sense of community, shared responsibility, and collective defense that factions provide can make all the difference in ensuring long-term survival and stability.

How to Form Your Own Group (7 Step Guide)

Forming your own survival group during an apocalyptic event can be both an adventure and a necessity. Here's a quirky and fun guide to get you started on building your own team of apocalypse-ready friends.

Step 1: Choose Your Dream Team

Think about who you'd want on your team. Maybe it's your best friend who can cook up a storm, your neighbor who's a DIY genius, or that quiet classmate who's secretly a martial arts expert. Diversity is key! You want a mix of skills and personalities to cover all bases. And don't forget about the pet – even a loyal dog can be a valuable member.

Step 2: Establish Roles

Now that you've got your squad, it's time to assign roles based on everyone's strengths. Here are a few fun roles to consider:

- The Scout: This person has a knack for finding the best routes and hidden resources.
- The Medic: With basic first aid knowledge, they keep everyone in top shape.
- The Builder: Handy with tools and creative, they can whip up shelters and fortifications.
- The Strategist: The brainiac who loves puzzles and planning, perfect for mapping out your survival strategy.
- The Forager: Expert in identifying edible plants and tracking down food sources.

"Teamwork makes the dream work"

Step 3: Create a Cool Name and Motto

Every great group needs an awesome name and a catchy motto. How about "The Apocalypse Avengers" with the motto "Survive and Thrive"? Or "The Undead Enders" with "Brains and Brawn"? Get creative and make it something everyone can rally behind.

Step 4: Establish a Headquarters

Your group needs a base of operations. Whether it's a treehouse, an underground bunker, or just a well-fortified living room, make it your own. Stock it with essentials like food, water, first aid kits, and entertainment. Decorate it with motivational posters and maps of your area for planning.

Step 5: Develop a Secret Language or Code

Having a secret language or code can be both fun and practical. Develop signals or phrases that only your group understands. This can help you communicate discreetly and keep your plans hidden from potential threats.

Step 6: Hold Training Sessions

Make training sessions fun and engaging. Turn survival skills into games and challenges. Who can build the best shelter in the shortest time? Who's the quickest at setting up a perimeter alarm? Practice makes perfect, and it's a great way to bond with your group.

"Survival isn't just about staying alive; it's about thriving together."

Step 7: Stay Flexible and Adapt

No plan is perfect, so stay flexible. Be ready to adapt your strategies as situations change. Hold regular meetings to discuss what's working and what needs improvement. Everyone's input is valuable.

"Adaptability is key to survival. If Plan A fails, remember there are 25 more letters in the alphabet!"

Historical Examples of Group Dynamics and Survival

- **The Shackleton Expedition**: In 1914, Sir Ernest Shackleton led an expedition to Antarctica that ended in disaster when their ship, the Endurance, was trapped and crushed by pack ice. Shackleton's exceptional leadership and the group's strong cohesion and shared goals ensured the survival of all 28 crew members through extreme conditions over nearly two years. Their unity and resourcefulness in the face of adversity are often cited as prime examples of the importance of effective group dynamics.

- **The Donner Party**: In 1846, a group of American pioneers traveling to California became stranded in the Sierra Nevada mountains during a brutal winter. Those who formed smaller, cohesive groups within the larger party, shared resources, and made collective decisions had higher survival rates. The tragic fate of the Donner Party underscores how vital cooperation and shared effort are in survival situations.

- **Apollo 13 Mission**: In 1970, the Apollo 13 mission to the moon faced a critical failure when an oxygen tank exploded. The astronauts' survival depended on their ability to work together seamlessly with mission control on Earth. Trust, clear communication, and collective problem-solving enabled the safe return of the crew. This event is a testament to the power of group dynamics and teamwork in crisis management.

- **The Siege of Leningrad**: During World War II, the city of Leningrad (now St. Petersburg) was besieged by Nazi forces for 872 days, from 1941 to 1944. The city's residents and defenders survived extreme conditions, including starvation and relentless attacks, by pooling resources, maintaining high morale, and organizing collective efforts to defend the city and sustain life. Their unity and resilience are remembered as remarkable examples of the strength found in effective group dynamics and leadership.

"Coming together is a beginning, staying together is progress, and working together is success." – Henry Ford

Building Your Way Up the Hierarchy

As you establish yourself as a competent and trustworthy leader, your influence will grow. Here's how you can continue to build your way up the hierarchy:

Adapt and Evolve:

- Continuously improve your skills and knowledge. Stay adaptable to changing circumstances and challenges.

Mentor Others:

- Develop potential leaders within your group. By mentoring others, you create a more robust and resilient community.

Expand Your Network:

- Form alliances with other factions. Building a network of allied groups can provide mutual support and increase your influence.

Lead with Compassion:

- Show empathy and understanding. A compassionate leader can inspire loyalty and foster a strong, united community.

By following these steps and continuously proving your leadership abilities, you can rise to the top of your camp's hierarchy. Effective leadership in a zombie apocalypse isn't just about survival—it's about creating a cohesive, motivated group capable of facing any challenge together.

How to Become a Camp Leader

Why Leadership is Crucial

In a post-apocalyptic world, leadership can mean the difference between chaos and survival. As populations descend into factions, strong, capable leaders are essential to guide groups through the challenges ahead. Becoming a camp leader involves earning the trust and respect of your group, demonstrating your abilities, and building a hierarchy that supports stability and growth.

The Descent into Factions

As society collapses during a zombie apocalypse, the once unified population will likely fragment into smaller groups or factions. These factions will form based on various factors:

- Survival Needs: People will band together to pool resources such as food, water, and shelter.
- Skill Sets: Groups may form around individuals with specific skills, such as medical knowledge, combat abilities, or survival expertise.
- Ideologies: Shared beliefs or goals, such as the desire to find a safe zone or rebuild society, can unite people into factions.
- Geographical Location: Proximity will naturally bring people together, leading to localized factions.

In this fragmented world, strong leadership is crucial. Here's how you can become a leader and build your way up the hierarchy:

Step 1: Demonstrate Competence

Knowledge and Skills:

- Survival Skills: Show proficiency in essential survival skills like finding food and water, building shelters, and defending against threats.

- Problem Solving: Demonstrate the ability to think on your feet and come up with creative solutions to unforeseen problems.
- Medical Knowledge: Basic first aid and medical skills can make you an invaluable member of the group.

Resource Management:

- Organize Resources: Take initiative in managing and distributing resources fairly and efficiently.
- Planning: Show foresight by creating plans for short-term survival and long-term sustainability.

Step 2: Earn Trust and Respect

Lead by Example:

- Work Ethic: Be willing to take on difficult tasks and share the workload.
- Integrity: Be honest and transparent with your group to build trust.

Communication:

- Listen Actively: Pay attention to the concerns and ideas of others.
- Speak Clearly: Communicate your plans and strategies effectively, ensuring everyone understands their roles and responsibilities.

Step 3: Build Alliances and Support

Form Relationships:

- Connect with Key Members: Identify individuals with influence or valuable skills and build strong relationships with them.
- Foster Team Spirit: Encourage cooperation and camaraderie within the group.

Conflict Resolution:

- Mediate Disputes: Step in to resolve conflicts fairly and diplomatically.
- Create a Fair System: Implement a system for addressing grievances and ensuring everyone feels heard.

Step 4: Establish a Hierarchical Structure

Create Roles:

- Delegate Tasks: Assign roles based on individuals' strengths and skills, such as scouts, medics, and defenders.
- Define Responsibilities: Clearly outline the duties and expectations for each role.

Implement Rules:

- Set Guidelines: Establish rules for behavior, resource allocation, and decision-making.
- Enforce Consistently: Ensure rules are applied fairly to maintain order and discipline.

Step 5: Show Vision and Direction

Set Goals:

- Short-Term Goals: Focus on immediate survival needs, such as securing food and fortifying the camp.
- Long-Term Vision: Develop a plan for future growth, safety, and possibly rebuilding society.

Inspire Hope:

- Positive Outlook: Keep morale high by maintaining a positive attitude and encouraging others.
- Lead with Confidence: Display confidence in your leadership to instill trust and motivate your group.

Fun Fact: Did You Know?

Did you know that during historical crises, communities have often turned to strong leaders who demonstrate competence and integrity? For example, during the Great Depression, leaders who showed empathy and provided clear direction were able to unite and guide their communities through tough times.

Setting Up Rules

Setting up rules and roles is crucial for maintaining order and ensuring everyone knows their responsibilities. As the camp leader, it's your job to establish clear guidelines that keep the group cohesive and functioning smoothly. Here's how to do it:

Step 1: Establish Clear Rules

Creating a set of rules helps manage expectations and reduces conflicts. These rules should be clear, concise, and agreed upon by everyone in the group.

1. Safety First: Establish protocols for handling dangerous situations, like encounters with wild animals or other groups.
2. Resource Management: Set guidelines for rationing food, water, and other essential supplies.
3. Hygiene Practices: Ensure everyone follows basic hygiene practices to prevent illness.
4. Conflict Resolution: Implement a system for resolving disputes peacefully.
5. Communication: Encourage open and honest communication among group members.

"In a survival situation, rules aren't just guidelines; they are lifelines."

Step 2: Establish Roles

Now that you've got your squad, it's time to assign roles based on everyone's strengths. Here are a few fun roles to consider:

1. The Scout: This person has a knack for finding the best routes and hidden resources.
2. The Medic: With basic first aid knowledge, they keep everyone in top shape.
3. The Builder: Handy with tools and creative, they can whip up shelters and fortifications.
4. The Strategist: The brainiac who loves puzzles and planning, perfect for mapping out your survival strategy.
5. The Forager: Expert in identifying edible plants and tracking down food sources.

Step 3: Regular Meetings

Hold regular group meetings to discuss plans, address concerns, and make decisions collectively. This fosters a sense of community and ensures everyone feels heard.

1. Daily Check-Ins: Brief meetings to go over the day's tasks and any issues that arose.
2. Weekly Strategy Sessions: Longer meetings to discuss long-term plans and reassess roles and rules as needed.

"The strength of the team is each individual member. The strength of each member is the team." - Phil Jackson

Step 4: Adaptability

Rules and roles should be flexible to adapt to changing situations. Encourage feedback from group members and be willing to make adjustments as necessary.

1. Feedback Loop: Create a system where group members can provide input on rules and roles.
2. Flexibility: Be prepared to shift roles if someone's strengths change or if new challenges arise.
3. Continuous Improvement: Regularly review and refine your rules and roles to ensure they remain effective.

True or False: Establishing a Successful Faction Group

Forming a successful faction group in a post-apocalyptic scenario requires a strategic approach. Below, we'll explore several statements about establishing and maintaining such a group. Determine whether each statement is true or false and learn the best practices for creating a thriving faction.

1. **True or False:** Regular emergency drills are unnecessary and create unnecessary panic within the group.
   False. Regular emergency drills are crucial for ensuring that everyone knows what to do in a crisis. Drills help to reinforce emergency protocols and improve the group's overall preparedness, reducing panic during real emergencies.

2. **True or False:** It's important to resolve conflicts quickly and quietly without involving the entire group.
   False. While swift conflict resolution is important, it's also essential to have a transparent process that the entire group understands. This prevents misunderstandings and ensures that all members feel heard and respected.

3. **True or False:** Managing resources effectively involves strict rationing and limiting access to essential supplies.
   True. Effective resource management often requires strict rationing to ensure supplies last. However, it's also important to communicate these measures clearly to the group and involve them in decision-making to maintain trust and cooperation.

4. **True or False:** Health and hygiene protocols can be relaxed once the initial threat has passed.
   False. Health and hygiene protocols should always be strictly followed to prevent illness and maintain the overall well-being of the group. Consistent hygiene practices are vital for long-term survival.

5. **True or False:** Establishing robust security and defense plans is more important than focusing on internal group dynamics.

   False. While security and defense are crucial, internal group dynamics are equally important. A group that works well together is more effective at implementing defense strategies and maintaining overall security.

6. **True or False:** Continuous learning and skill development are luxuries that can be ignored in a survival situation.

   False. Continuous learning and skill development are essential for adapting to new challenges and improving the group's chances of survival. Teaching and learning new skills keeps the group versatile and prepared for any situation.

7. **True or False:** Reliable communication systems are essential for maintaining coordination and safety within the group.

   True. Reliable communication systems are vital for effective coordination, ensuring that all members are informed and can respond quickly to any threats or changes in plans.

8. **8. True or False:** It is beneficial to establish alliances with other groups when possible.

   True. Alliances with other groups can provide mutual benefits such as resource sharing, increased security, and broader support networks. However, it's important to choose allies carefully and establish clear terms for cooperation.

Chapter 5: Building an Outpost

What is an Outpost?

An outpost is a strategically positioned base or station established by a group for various purposes, including surveillance, defense, and resource management. It acts as a forward position that can provide early warnings, facilitate communication, and serve as a hub for operations. In apocalyptic scenarios such as civil wars, zombie outbreaks, or other end-of-world situations, outposts become crucial for survival and tactical advantages.

Why We Need an Outpost

Surveillance and Early Warning

An outpost allows for constant monitoring of surrounding areas, which is essential for detecting potential threats early. Whether it's a zombie horde, hostile human factions, or approaching natural disasters, an outpost provides the necessary vantage point to observe and react to dangers before they reach the main group.

Example: During a zombie apocalypse, an outpost can monitor zombie movements and alert the main camp, giving them enough time to fortify defenses or evacuate if necessary.

Resource Management and Expansion

Outposts can be strategically placed near valuable resources such as water sources, food supplies, or medical facilities. By establishing control over these resources, a group can ensure a steady supply of essentials, reducing the need to travel long distances from the main base.

Communication and Coordination

Outposts serve as relay points for communication, especially in areas where direct communication might be difficult. They can be equipped with radios, signal flares, or other communication tools to maintain constant contact with the main base and other outposts.

Defense and Security

Outposts act as the first line of defense against any threats. They can be fortified to withstand attacks, providing a buffer zone that protects the main camp. This layered defense strategy makes it harder for enemies or zombies to breach the main base.

Staging Area for Operations

Outposts can function as staging areas for various operations, including reconnaissance missions, rescue efforts, or attacks on hostile groups. They provide a secure location to plan, rest, and resupply before executing missions.

Example: In a civil war, an outpost near enemy territory allows a group to conduct surveillance and plan strategic strikes with a safe fallback position.

Psychological Advantage

Having well-established outposts can boost the morale of the group. It gives a sense of control over the territory and provides safe havens for members to retreat to if needed. This psychological edge can be crucial in maintaining group cohesion and resilience.

Crazy Facts

- Ancient Outposts: The Romans established outposts called "castella" along their empire's borders to monitor and defend against invasions.

- Wild West: During the American frontier expansion, outposts were critical for settlers, providing protection against native tribes and facilitating communication across vast distances.
- Military Use: Modern militaries use forward operating bases (FOBs) as outposts to launch operations and maintain supply lines in hostile territories.
- Space Exploration: NASA is planning outposts on the Moon and Mars to serve as bases for extended exploration and potential colonization.
- Historical Sieges: During medieval sieges, outposts were often used to cut off supplies to the besieged city, forcing them into submission.
- Arctic Exploration: Early Arctic explorers set up outposts to survive harsh conditions and as starting points for further exploration.
- WWII: During WWII, the Allies established outposts in remote locations to monitor enemy movements and coordinate attacks.
- Science Fiction: In many sci-fi stories, outposts on distant planets serve as humanity's first line of defense against alien threats.
- Pirate Havens: Pirates used hidden outposts in the Caribbean to stash loot, repair ships, and plan attacks on merchant vessels.
- Modern Survivalists: Today, some survivalists and preppers build remote outposts stocked with supplies as part of their emergency preparedness plans.

How to Build a Strong Fort

"An ounce of prevention is worth a pound of cure." – Benjamin Franklin

In any apocalyptic scenario, a strong fort can be the difference between life and death. The primary purpose of a fort is to provide a secure base of operations, offering protection from external threats and a safe place for rest and recovery. Here's how to build a robust fort that can withstand both human and zombie threats.

Foundation and Materials: The foundation of your fort is critical. Choose a location that offers natural defense advantages, such as a hilltop or an area surrounded by natural barriers like rivers or cliffs. Use durable materials such as concrete, brick, or heavy timber to construct the walls. Reinforce the walls with steel beams or rebar to increase their strength. Ensure the base is deep and solid to prevent easy collapse or penetration.

Design and Layout: Design your fort with multiple layers of defense. Include high walls, watchtowers, and a secure gate. Inside the fort, create separate zones for living, storage, and defense operations. Incorporate escape routes and hidden bunkers as a last line of defense. Ensure there are enough windows and lookout points for surveillance but secure them with bars or reinforced shutters to prevent entry.

Tips and Tricks:

1. **Moat and Barriers:** Dig a moat or create barriers around your fort to slow down attackers.
2. **Multi-Layered Walls:** Use double walls with a gap filled with gravel or spikes to deter climbing.
3. **Camouflage:** Use natural materials to blend your fort into the environment, making it less noticeable.
4. **Booby Traps:** Set up traps around the perimeter to catch intruders off guard.
5. **Elevated Platforms:** Build platforms for lookouts and archers to defend from a height advantage.

"The only safe ship in a storm is leadership."
— Faye Wattleton

Setting Up Watchtowers

"The best way to predict the future is to create it." –
Peter Drucker

Watchtowers are essential for maintaining vigilance and providing early warnings of approaching threats. They allow you to monitor a wide area, giving you the upper hand in spotting and responding to dangers.

Construction and Placement: Build your watchtowers with sturdy materials like wood or metal, ensuring they are tall enough to provide a clear view of the surrounding area. Place watchtowers at key points around your perimeter, such as corners or elevated spots. Ensure they are interconnected with the main fort via secure pathways or tunnels.

Functionality and Equipment: Equip your watchtowers with powerful binoculars, spotlights, and communication devices. Install alarm systems that can be triggered to alert the main fort of any imminent threats. Stock each tower with emergency supplies, including weapons, first aid kits, and a secure place for lookouts to rest.

Tips and Tricks:

1. **360-Degree View:** Ensure each watchtower provides a complete 360-degree view for comprehensive surveillance.
2. **Communication Lines:** Set up reliable communication lines between towers and the main fort.
3. **Redundant Systems:** Have backup power sources like solar panels or batteries for equipment in the watchtowers.
4. **Night Vision:** Equip towers with night vision goggles or infrared cameras for nighttime monitoring.
5. **Rotation Shifts:** Establish a rotation system for lookout duties to keep everyone alert and rested.

"Forewarned is forearmed."

Creating a Safe Perimeter

A well-defined and secure perimeter is your first line of defense against external threats. It serves as a buffer zone that can delay or deter attackers, giving you crucial time to respond.

Fencing and Barriers: Construct a strong fence using materials like steel, barbed wire, or reinforced wood. The fence should be tall and difficult to climb, with additional deterrents like electric wiring or spikes. Surround the fence with natural barriers like thorny bushes or ditches filled with sharp objects.

Surveillance and Patrol: Constant surveillance and regular patrols are key to maintaining a secure perimeter. Use cameras, motion sensors, and tripwires to detect intruders. Organize patrol teams to walk the perimeter at regular intervals, ensuring there are no weak spots or breaches.

Tips and Tricks:

1. **Layered Defenses:** Create multiple layers of barriers for added security.
2. **Clear Line of Sight:** Keep the area around the perimeter clear of obstructions to prevent hiding spots for intruders.
3. **Light Up:** Install bright lights around the perimeter to deter night-time approaches.
4. **Sound Alarms:** Use noise-making devices like bells or sirens to alert you to breaches.
5. **Guard Animals:** Train dogs or other animals to patrol and alert you to unusual activities.

"The greatest fine art of the future will be the making of a comfortable living from a small piece of land." – Abraham Lincoln

Growing Your Own Food

In a long-term survival scenario, growing your own food is essential for sustainability and health. Establishing a reliable food source reduces dependence on scavenging and ensures a steady supply of nutrients.

Choosing the Right Crops: Select crops that are easy to grow and have a high yield. Consider staples like potatoes, beans, corn, and hardy greens such as kale or spinach. Fruits like berries or apples can provide essential vitamins. Focus on crops that can be preserved or stored for long periods.

Setting Up the Garden: Choose a sunny location with good soil drainage for your garden. Use raised beds or containers if the soil quality is poor. Implement composting to enrich the soil with nutrients. Install a reliable water source, such as a rainwater collection system or an irrigation setup. Protect your garden with fencing to keep out pests and animals.

Tips and Tricks:

1. **Companion Planting:** Plant crops that benefit each other, such as beans with corn, to maximize yield.
2. **Seed Saving:** Learn to save seeds from your crops to replant in future seasons.
3. **Vertical Gardening:** Use trellises and vertical spaces to grow climbing plants and maximize space.
4. **Greenhouses:** Build a greenhouse to extend the growing season and protect plants from harsh weather.
5. **Natural Pest Control:** Use natural methods like introducing beneficial insects or using homemade sprays to keep pests at bay.

By incorporating these strategies into your survival plan, you can ensure a fortified base, effective surveillance, a secure perimeter, and a sustainable food supply, significantly increasing your chances of thriving in any apocalyptic scenario.

The World's Most Famous Forts

Forts have played a crucial role in human history, serving as defensive structures, symbols of power, and centers of governance. They have witnessed countless battles, political changes, and historical events. Here's a look at some of the world's most famous forts, their unique features, and historical significance.

The Great Wall of China

Not a single fort, but a series of fortifications made of stone, brick, tamped earth, wood, and other materials.

- Built to protect the northern borders of the Chinese Empire against various nomadic groups. Stretches over 13,000 miles, including walls, watchtowers, and barracks.
- The Great Wall is often mistakenly believed to be visible from space with the naked eye, but it is not.

> "He who has not climbed the Great Wall is not a true man." – Mao Zedong

Fort Knox (United States)

A United States Army post in Kentucky, best known as the site of the United States Bullion Depository.

- Holds a significant portion of the U.S. gold reserves and has become synonymous with high security. The vault is made of steel plates, steel beams, and concrete, making it one of the most secure places on Earth.
- Fort Knox has never been robbed, and its security measures are highly classified.

> "The safest place in the world, yet the most unassuming."

The Tower of London (United Kingdom)

A historic castle located on the north bank of the River Thames in central London.

- Served as a royal residence, prison, and treasury. It is now home to the Crown Jewels of England. Famous for its Yeoman Warders (Beefeaters) and the legend of the ravens.
- The Tower of London has seen its fair share of intrigue, from royal prisoners to executions.

"The Tower is a symbol of power, cruelty, and mystery."

Red Fort (India)

A historic fort in Delhi that served as the main residence of the Mughal emperors.

- Site of major historical events, including the first independence day celebrations of India. Known for its massive enclosing walls of red sandstone and its blend of Persian, Timurid, and Indian architecture.
- The fort houses several museums that document India's rich history and struggle for independence.

"The epitome of grandeur and history."

Alhambra (Spain)

A palace and fortress complex located in Granada, Andalusia, Spain.

- Served as the residence of the Moorish monarchs and their court. Known for its stunning Islamic architecture, intricate stucco work, and beautiful gardens.
- Alhambra means "The Red One," referring to the color of the clay used in its construction.

"A pearl set in emeralds." – Moorish poets

Chapter 6: Creating a New Society

Building a Trading System

By implementing this economic plan, we can create a stable and prosperous society in the aftermath of any apocalyptic event. Our new currency and trade system will foster cooperation, build trust, and ensure that all factions can thrive together in this challenging new world.

Step 1: Establishing Trust and Cooperation

Create a Council of Leaders:

- Form a council with representatives from different factions to discuss and agree on the new economic plan. This will ensure that the system is fair and benefits all parties involved.
- Promote open communication and transparency to build trust among the factions.

Define the New Currency:

- **Barter System:** Initially, trade will rely heavily on bartering goods and services. This is the most immediate and straightforward method of exchange.
- **Commodity-Based Currency:** Over time, introduce a commodity-based currency. Items with intrinsic value and universal need, such as food, medical supplies, ammunition, and tools, can serve as the basis for this currency.
- **Token System:** Create physical tokens or digital credits that represent the value of these commodities. These tokens can

be exchanged and used as currency within and between factions.

Step 2: Establishing the Currency

Identify Valuable Commodities:

Determine which items are most valuable and universally needed. These might include:

- Food (canned goods, dried foods)
- Water purification tablets
- Medical supplies (bandages, antibiotics)
- Ammunition
- Tools and equipment

Minting Tokens:

- **Physical Tokens:** Use durable materials like metal or plastic to create tokens that represent specific values of commodities. Each token should be easily recognizable and difficult to counterfeit.
- **Digital Credits:** If technology permits, create a secure digital currency system. Use simple, secure methods like QR codes or encrypted apps to manage and transfer credits.

Example Currency Names:

- Zombucks
- Survivor Coins
- Resilience Tokens
- Barter Bits
- Apoca-credits
- Undead Units
- Sanctuary Silver
- Phoenix Points
- Revival Credits
- Survival Shillings
- Fortitude Funds

- Necro Notes
- Haven Tokens
- Outpost Gold

Step 3: Setting Up Trade Systems

Establish Trade Centers:

- Set up designated trade centers or markets where factions can meet to exchange goods and services. These centers should be secure and neutral grounds.
- Appoint trusted individuals to oversee the trade centers and ensure fair trading practices.

Create Trade Agreements:

- Negotiate trade agreements between factions to ensure a steady flow of goods and services. These agreements should outline the terms of trade, including acceptable commodities, exchange rates, and dispute resolution mechanisms.

Implement Fair Trade Practices:

- Establish and enforce rules to prevent exploitation and ensure fair trading. This includes setting standard prices for common goods and services to avoid price gouging.
- Create a system for resolving disputes and handling fraud or theft.

Step 4: Encouraging Economic Growth

Incentivize Production:

- Encourage the production of valuable commodities by offering rewards or incentives. For example, factions that produce surplus food or medical supplies could receive extra tokens or credits.
- Promote skills training and knowledge sharing to increase productivity and self-sufficiency.

Foster Innovation and Entrepreneurship:

- Support initiatives and projects that contribute to the overall well-being and economic stability of the community. This could include new farming techniques, medical innovations, or improved security measures.
- Provide resources and support for entrepreneurs who come up with innovative solutions to common problems.

Step 5: Maintaining Stability

Monitor and Adjust:

- Regularly monitor the economic system to ensure it is functioning smoothly. Be prepared to make adjustments as needed to address issues such as inflation, scarcity, or inequity.
- Use feedback from the council of leaders and the community to make informed decisions.

Build Reserves:

- Establish reserves of essential commodities to buffer against shortages and crises. This can help maintain stability and trust in the economic system.
- Encourage each faction to contribute to and maintain their own reserves.

Educate the Community:

- Educate community members about the new currency and trade system. Ensure everyone understands how it works and the benefits it provides.
- Promote financial literacy and responsible trading practices.

Did you know that during times of crisis in history, communities have often reverted to barter systems and commodity-based currencies? For example, during World War II, cigarettes became a popular form of currency among soldiers and civilians due to their high value and widespread demand.

- Within correctional facilities, prisoners often resort to using commodity-based currencies for trade. Items like instant noodles, toiletries, and even postage stamps have been used as currency among inmates to facilitate transactions within the prison economy.
- In post-apocalyptic literature and media, authors frequently explore the concept of alternative currencies arising after societal collapse. These currencies can range from practical items like ammunition or fuel to more symbolic forms of value, such as bottle caps in the Fallout video game series.
- Zimbabwe faced hyperinflation in the late 2000s, leading to the abandonment of the local currency, the Zimbabwean dollar. During this time, bartering became a common practice as people sought alternative ways to acquire essential items. Goods like agricultural produce, livestock, and household goods were frequently traded in local markets and informal exchanges.

Chapter 6: Creating a New Society

Setting Up a Political System

In a post-apocalyptic world, establishing a political system is crucial for maintaining order, ensuring fairness, and fostering a sense of community. Here are a few quirky and fun political systems to consider for your new society. Each option comes with its own unique flavor and advantages. Choose the one that best fits your group's needs and values!

- Democracy
- Meritocracy
- Oligarchy
- Tribal System
- Technocracy
- Anarcho-Communism

- Monarchy
- Theocratic

1. Democracy: Power to the People

Democracy is a system where all members of the community have a say in decision-making. Leaders are elected by the people, and major decisions are made through voting.

How It Works:

- **Elections:** Hold regular elections to choose representatives and leaders. Ensure that the process is fair, transparent, and accessible to all eligible members.
- **Voting:** Implement various voting methods, such as majority voting for general decisions and ranked-choice voting for elections.
- **Council of Leaders:** Form a governing council with representatives from different factions to oversee operations and make decisions.

Facts

1. **Ancient Athens:** Ancient Athens is often credited with developing the first known democracy, where citizens voted directly on legislation and executive bills.
2. **Magna Carta:** The Magna Carta, signed in 1215, is considered one of the first steps towards modern democracy. It limited the powers of the king and established certain legal protections for subjects.
3. **World's Oldest Democracy:** Iceland claims to have the world's oldest functioning democracy, with its parliament, the Althing, established in 930 AD.
4. **Swiss Direct Democracy:** Switzerland practices a form of direct democracy, where citizens can propose changes to the constitution and vote on national referendums.
5. **American Democracy:** The United States is one of the oldest modern democracies, with its Constitution established

in 1787. It introduced a system of checks and balances among the executive, legislative, and judicial branches.

6. **Universal Suffrage:** New Zealand was the first self-governing country to grant all adult women the right to vote in parliamentary elections in 1893.

7. **Indian Democracy:** India is the largest democracy in the world, with over 900 million eligible voters participating in its general elections.

8. **Secret Ballot:** Australia was the first country to implement the secret ballot in 1856, ensuring that voters could cast their votes privately without fear of intimidation.

9. **Town Hall Meetings:** In some parts of New England, town hall meetings are a direct democratic practice where local residents gather to discuss and vote on community issues.

10. **Digital Democracy:** Estonia is a pioneer in digital democracy, offering online voting for its citizens since 2005, making it one of the first countries to embrace e-democracy on a national level.

"Democracy is the worst form of government, except for all the others." - Winston Churchill

2. Meritocracy: Rule by the Most Capable

Meritocracy is a system where individuals are selected for positions of authority based on their abilities and merits rather than their wealth or social status.

How It Works:

- **Skills Assessment:** Conduct assessments to identify the strengths and skills of each community member.
- **Leadership Positions:** Assign leadership roles based on expertise and demonstrated ability.
- **Performance Reviews:** Regularly review the performance of leaders and make adjustments as needed.

"Meritocracy ensures that the best and brightest are guiding our society."

Facts

- The concept of meritocracy was popularized by the Chinese Imperial Examination system, where scholars were selected for government positions based on their knowledge and abilities.
- Besides the Chinese Imperial Examination system, meritocratic principles were also evident in ancient Greece, where positions in certain city-states were awarded based on merit and accomplishments rather than birthright.
- In modern times, meritocracy is often seen in corporate environments, where employees are promoted based on performance, skills, and contributions rather than tenure or personal connections.
- Meritocratic systems place a high value on education and continuous learning, encouraging individuals to improve their skills and knowledge to advance in their roles. This focus on education helps to ensure that leaders are well-prepared to handle complex challenges.

3. Oligarchy: Rule by a Few

Oligarchy is a system where a small group of people, often distinguished by royalty, wealth, family ties, or military control, hold power and make decisions for the society.

How It Works:

- **Selection of Leaders:** Choose a small group of individuals with significant influence or expertise to lead.
- **Council Meetings:** The ruling group holds regular meetings to discuss and make decisions.
- **Accountability:** Implement checks and balances to ensure that the ruling group acts in the best interest of the community.

"Oligarchy works best when the few in power are wise and just." – Plato

Facts

- **Wealth-Based Power:** In many historical oligarchies, power was concentrated in the hands of the wealthy elite. This often led to significant economic disparities within the society.
- **Family Dynasties:** Oligarchies often feature powerful family dynasties, where leadership roles are passed down through generations, maintaining power within a select group.
- **Corporate Oligarchy:** In some modern contexts, oligarchies can take the form of corporate power, where a few large corporations or wealthy individuals have significant influence over political decisions and policies.
- **Roman Republic:** The Roman Republic had elements of an oligarchy with its Senate, where power was held by a small group of patrician families who influenced major decisions and policies.
- **Venetian Oligarchy:** The Republic of Venice operated under an oligarchic system where the Doge was elected by the city's elite, and decision-making power was concentrated among the wealthy merchant families.
- **Modern Examples:** Some critics argue that certain contemporary nations exhibit oligarchic tendencies, where political power is concentrated among a small group of influential individuals or families, despite formal democratic structures.

4. Tribal System: Back to Basics

A tribal system is based on traditional, often familial, groups led by elders or chiefs. This system emphasizes communal living, shared resources, and collective decision-making.

How It Works:

- **Clan Formation:** Organize the community into clans or tribes based on kinship or common interests.
- **Elder Council:** Each tribe is led by a council of elders or chiefs who are respected for their wisdom and experience.
- **Consensus Decision-Making:** Decisions are made through consensus within the tribe, ensuring that everyone's voice is heard.

"In the tribal system, the strength of the community is built on the wisdom of the elders." – Native American Proverb

Many indigenous cultures around the world have used tribal systems for centuries, valuing the wisdom of their elders and the strength of their communal bonds.

Facts

- Kinship Bonds: In tribal systems, kinship bonds form the foundation of social organization. These ties are crucial for maintaining loyalty and cooperation among members.
- Resource Sharing: Tribes often operate on principles of communal resource sharing, ensuring that everyone has access to the necessities for survival. This promotes a strong sense of community and mutual support.
- Rituals and Traditions: Tribal societies place a high value on rituals and traditions, which help to reinforce social cohesion and cultural identity. These practices are passed down through generations and play a key role in decision-making and conflict resolution.
- Land Stewardship: Many tribal systems practice sustainable land stewardship, viewing themselves as caretakers of the land rather than owners. This perspective often leads to practices that are environmentally sustainable and respect the natural world.

- Conflict Resolution: Traditional tribal systems often employ unique methods of conflict resolution, such as mediation by respected elders or community-wide discussions, to maintain harmony and avoid violence. These practices emphasize reconciliation and collective well-being.

5. Technocracy: Rule by the Experts

Technocracy is a system where decision-makers are selected based on their expertise in specific areas, such as science and technology, rather than political affiliations or personal wealth.

How It Works:

- **Identify Experts:** Select leaders who have specialized knowledge and skills relevant to the community's needs.
- **Advisory Committees:** Form committees of experts in various fields (e.g., agriculture, medicine, engineering) to provide advice and make decisions.
- **Data-Driven Decisions:** Use scientific data and research to guide policy-making and problem-solving.

> "In a technocracy, the right knowledge leads to the right decisions." – Alvin Toffler

The term "technocracy" was coined in the early 20th century and has been explored in various forms of speculative fiction, envisioning societies where technical experts make key decisions.

6. Anarcho-Communism: Shared Power, Shared Resources

Anarcho-communism is a system where there is no centralized government. Instead, all property is communally owned, and decisions are made collectively through direct democracy.

How It Works:

- **Collective Ownership:** All resources and property are shared among the community members.

- **Direct Democracy:** Decisions are made through general assemblies where everyone has a voice and a vote.
- **Voluntary Cooperation:** People work together voluntarily, based on mutual aid and cooperation, rather than coercion.

"From each according to their ability, to each according to their need." – Karl Marx

Anarcho-communism has been practiced in various forms throughout history, notably in certain indigenous societies and during the Spanish Civil War in the 1930s.

Facts

- **Karl Marx's Influence:** Although Karl Marx is more commonly associated with communism, his ideas on a stateless, classless society where resources are shared according to need have heavily influenced anarcho-communist thought.
- **Historical Anarcho-Communism:** The Makhnovist movement in Ukraine (1917-1921), led by Nestor Makhno, is another historical example of anarcho-communism. This movement emphasized collective ownership and direct democracy in the face of both external and internal threats.
- **Anarchist Catalonia:** During the Spanish Civil War (1936-1939), parts of Catalonia were governed by anarcho-communist principles, with factories, farms, and services being collectively managed by workers and communities.
- **Modern Examples:** Contemporary examples of anarcho-communism can be found in various intentional communities and eco-villages around the world, where residents practice communal living and decision-making.
- **Voluntary Associations:** In anarcho-communist societies, individuals form voluntary associations for mutual benefit,

relying on cooperation rather than hierarchical structures to meet their needs.

- **Criticism and Debate:** Anarcho-communism faces criticism for its perceived lack of structure and potential challenges in large-scale implementation. Debates within the movement often focus on how to balance individual freedom with collective responsibility.

7. Monarchy: A Single Sovereign Leader

Monarchy is a system where a single individual, usually a king or queen, holds supreme power, often justified by tradition or divine right.

How It Works:

- **Selection of Monarch:** The leader is chosen through hereditary succession or by appointment.
- **Royal Court:** The monarch is supported by a court of advisors and nobles who help govern.
- **Absolute vs. Constitutional:** Decide whether the monarchy will be absolute (complete control) or constitutional (power shared with a legislative body).

"The king is the first servant of the state." – Frederick the Great

Facts

- Many of the world's oldest civilizations, including Ancient Egypt and Medieval Europe, were ruled by monarchies, where kings and queens wielded significant power.
- While many traditional monarchies still exist today, particularly in Europe and the Middle East, some have transitioned to constitutional monarchies, where the monarch's powers are limited by a constitution and democratic institutions. Examples include the United Kingdom, Japan, and Spain.

- Monarchies are often characterized by elaborate ceremonies and rituals that symbolize the authority and legitimacy of the ruler. These may include coronations, investitures, and state banquets, which serve to reinforce the monarch's position as the head of state.
- monarchs are passed down through generations within a ruling family. This system often places importance on lineage and bloodlines, with the eldest child or closest relative typically inheriting the throne.

8. Theocratic Rule: Guided by Spiritual Leaders

Theocracy is a system where religious leaders govern, and the laws are based on religious doctrines.

How It Works:

- **Religious Council:** Form a council of religious leaders who interpret and enforce laws based on sacred texts.
- **Moral Governance:** Ensure that the policies and decisions align with the community's spiritual beliefs and values.
- **Community Guidance:** Provide spiritual and moral guidance to maintain social harmony and ethical behavior.

"In a theocracy, faith and governance are intertwined."

- Throughout history, theocratic rule has been prominent in various cultures, such as Ancient Egypt, where pharaohs were considered gods, and in the Vatican City, governed by the Pope.
- In theocratic systems, religious leaders often claim to derive their authority directly from a deity or divine source. This belief in divine mandate provides legitimacy to the rule of religious leaders and justifies their governance based on religious principles.
- Theocracies typically enforce legal codes derived from religious scriptures or teachings. These codes prescribe

moral conduct, regulate social behavior, and adjudicate disputes according to religious doctrines. Examples include Sharia law in Islamic theocracies and Halakha in Jewish theocratic societies.

- Theocratic rule can face challenges in pluralistic societies where there are diverse religious beliefs and practices. Maintaining social cohesion and ensuring equal rights for all citizens, regardless of their faith, can be complex in such contexts, leading to tensions between religious and secular interests.

Chapter 7: Extreme Weather & Stuck in the Wild Survival

"Nature's fury is just another chapter in your adventure book."

"Snowstorms and heatwaves are like plot twists—unexpected but thrilling."

"When thunder roars, let your survival skills soar."

Surviving a Fall into a Cold Lake

Falling into a cold lake can be a shock to your system, and immediate action is crucial for survival. The icy water quickly saps your body heat, leading to hypothermia if you don't act fast.

"In icy waters, stay calm and let your survival instincts float to the surface."

1. Stay Calm and Float:

- Avoid Panic: Panicking wastes energy and accelerates heat loss. Try to stay calm and focus on your next steps.
- Float on Your Back: If you can't immediately find a way out, float on your back to conserve energy and keep your head above water.

2. Get Out Quickly:

- Find an Exit Point: Look for the closest shore or a solid object to grab onto, such as a dock or a sturdy branch.

- Use the Ice: If you fell through ice, use your elbows to pull yourself up. Kick your feet to propel your body onto the ice surface.

3. Remove Wet Clothing:

- Dry Off Immediately: Once out of the water, remove wet clothing as they draw heat away from your body. Replace with dry clothing or wrap yourself in any dry material available.
- Warm Up Slowly: Avoid rapid rewarming with hot water or fires; instead, use body heat, blankets, and dry clothes to gradually raise your body temperature.

Crazy Facts

- Did you know that the average person can survive in 32°F (0°C) water for only about 15 minutes before losing consciousness due to hypothermia? Quick action is crucial!
- When you plunge into cold water, your body activates the mammalian dive reflex, slowing your heart rate and conserving oxygen to help you survive longer underwater.
- Water conducts heat away from your body 25 times faster than air of the same temperature. That's why hypothermia sets in so quickly in cold water!

"A plunge into the cold can freeze your body, but not your will to survive."

Avoiding Hypothermia and Frostbite

Hypothermia and frostbite are serious risks in cold weather. Hypothermia occurs when your body loses heat faster than it can produce it, while frostbite is the freezing of skin and underlying tissues.

"Keep moving, stay dry, and outsmart the frost."

1. Recognize the Signs:

- Hypothermia: Symptoms include intense shivering, slurred speech, confusion, and loss of coordination.
- Frostbite: Look for numbness, white or grayish-yellow skin, and a hard or waxy feel to the affected area.

2. Dress Appropriately:

- Layer Up: Wear multiple layers of clothing to trap heat. Start with a moisture-wicking base layer, add an insulating layer, and finish with a waterproof outer layer.
- Protect Extremities: Wear insulated gloves, thick socks, and a hat. Use a scarf or balaclava to cover your face.

3. Stay Dry:

- Avoid Wet Conditions: Wet clothes lose their insulating properties, so stay as dry as possible. Use waterproof gear and change out of wet clothes immediately.
- Create a Barrier: Use a ground tarp or insulated pad to stay off wet or cold ground.

4. Seek Shelter:

- Wind Protection: Wind accelerates heat loss, so find or create a shelter that protects you from the wind. Use natural windbreaks like rocks or trees if necessary.
- Insulate Your Shelter: Line your shelter with leaves, pine needles, or other natural materials to provide additional insulation.

Crazy Facts

- Frostbite was a significant issue for soldiers during the Napoleonic Wars and World War II, leading to countless casualties from cold injuries.

- The coldest temperature ever recorded on Earth was -128.6°F (-89.2°C) at Vostok Station, Antarctica. Imagine surviving those conditions!
- In extreme cold, your body can undergo supercooling, where tissues remain unfrozen below their normal freezing point, potentially leading to severe frostbite without immediate signs.

"In the battle against the cold, preparation is your strongest ally."

Safe Ways to Cross Snow and Ice

Crossing snow and ice can be treacherous if you're not prepared. Proper techniques and caution can prevent falls and other accidents.

"Step lightly and wisely on snow and ice to avoid nature's hidden traps."

1. Assess the Terrain:

- Check the Ice Thickness: Before stepping onto ice, ensure it is thick enough to support your weight. Clear ice should be at least 4 inches thick for walking.
- Look for Signs of Weak Ice: Avoid areas with flowing water, cracks, or bubbles under the surface.

2. Use the Right Gear:

- Footwear: Wear boots with good traction or use crampons to improve grip on ice. For deep snow, use snowshoes to distribute your weight and prevent sinking.
- Poles and Probes: Carry trekking poles or ice probes to test the ice's thickness and stability ahead of you.

3. Move with Caution:

- Distribute Weight: Spread your weight evenly by crawling or lying flat on the ice if it appears unstable.
- Walk Slowly: Take small, deliberate steps to maintain balance and avoid sudden movements that could lead to falls.

4. Create a Safety Plan:

- Travel with a Partner: Always cross snow and ice with a companion. Keep a safe distance from each other to avoid both falling through the ice at once.
- Carry Rescue Equipment: Bring a rope, ice picks, and a flotation device to help rescue anyone who might fall through the ice.

Crazy Facts

- Record Ice Thickness: The thickest ice ever recorded was found on the Antarctic ice sheet, measuring an astonishing 15,669 feet (4,776 meters) thick. That's more than three miles of solid ice!
- Miracle Escape: In 2002, a woman in Sweden survived for nearly 80 minutes underwater in a frozen lake, with her body temperature dropping to 56°F (13.7°C). She was revived without any lasting brain damage, showcasing the body's incredible ability to survive in extreme cold.
- Vehicle Crossing: In some remote areas, ice roads are created on frozen lakes and rivers, allowing trucks and cars to drive across them. The world's longest ice road, the Tuktoyaktuk Winter Road in Canada, stretches over 120 miles (193 kilometers) and can support the weight of fully loaded trucks!

"In winter's frozen world, your steps must be as careful as they are confident."

Constructing Snow Shelters

Imagine you and your friends are on a winter hiking trip in the mountains. The sky was clear when you set out, but by late afternoon, dark clouds begin to gather, and snow starts falling heavily. Realizing that you won't make it back to your campsite before nightfall, you decide to construct a snow shelter to protect yourselves from the worsening storm. The temperature drops rapidly, and the wind picks up, making it clear that immediate action is necessary.

1. Choosing and Building Your Shelter

You decide to build a Quinzhee, as the snow in the area is loose and plentiful. You and your friends start by piling snow into a large mound, roughly six feet high and wide. You compact the snow by walking on it, and then let it settle for a couple of hours to ensure it's sturdy enough to hollow out. As you wait, you gather more snow for backup and share tips on efficient snow shelter construction. Once the snow has settled, you dig an entrance on the downhill side and carefully hollow out the mound, ensuring the walls and roof are at least 1-2 feet thick to provide adequate insulation and structural integrity.

2. Making It Livable

With the Quinzhee hollowed out, you make a small ventilation hole at the top to prevent carbon monoxide buildup from your breath. Next, you focus on making the interior as comfortable as possible. Using pine boughs and spare clothing, you line the floor to create a barrier against the cold ground. You also fashion a small, elevated sleeping platform to keep your body off the coldest part of the shelter. To further reduce the wind's chilling effect, you partially block the entrance with a backpack or a block of snow, allowing just enough space for air circulation.

3. Settling In for the Night

As the snowstorm rages outside, you and your friends huddle inside your makeshift Quinzhee, appreciating the relative warmth and protection it offers. The process of building the shelter has not only kept you physically active and warm but has also strengthened your teamwork and camaraderie. Inside, you share stories and keep each other entertained while you wait out the storm. You even try to melt some snow in a container with body heat to have extra drinking water. By the time the storm subsides, your Quinzhee has proven to be a reliable refuge, showcasing the importance of knowledge, preparedness, and cooperation in extreme weather conditions.

"In the heart of a snowstorm, a well-built shelter is not just a refuge—it's a testament to your ingenuity and teamwork."

Avoiding and Treating Sunburn and Heatstroke

In hot weather, sunburn and heatstroke are serious risks. Knowing how to prevent and treat these conditions can help you stay safe and healthy.

1. Avoiding Sunburn:

- Wear Protective Clothing: Long-sleeved shirts, wide-brimmed hats, and sunglasses can shield your skin from harmful UV rays.
- Use Sunscreen: Apply a broad-spectrum sunscreen with at least SPF 30. Reapply every two hours, or more frequently if sweating or swimming.
- Seek Shade: Avoid direct sunlight during peak hours (10 a.m. to 4 p.m.). Use natural shade or create your own with tarps or umbrellas.

2. Treating Sunburn:

- Cool the Skin: Apply cool, wet compresses or take a cool bath to soothe the burned skin.
- Moisturize: Use aloe vera gel or a moisturizing lotion to keep the skin hydrated and reduce peeling.
- Stay Hydrated: Drink plenty of fluids to help your skin recover and to prevent dehydration.

3. Avoiding Heatstroke:

- Stay Hydrated: Drink water regularly, even if you don't feel thirsty. Avoid caffeine and alcohol as they can lead to dehydration.
- Dress Appropriately: Wear lightweight, loose-fitting, and light-colored clothing to reflect sunlight and stay cool.
- Take Breaks: Rest in shaded or cool areas, and avoid strenuous activities during the hottest parts of the day.

4. Treating Heatstroke:

- Cool the Body: Move to a cool or shaded area. Apply cold packs to the neck, armpits, and groin, or immerse the body in cool water.
- Rehydrate: Drink cool water or sports drinks to replenish electrolytes.
- Seek Medical Attention: Heatstroke is a medical emergency. Get professional help as soon as possible.

In extreme heat, staying cool is crucial to prevent heat exhaustion or heatstroke. Here are some effective techniques to keep your body temperature down:

1. Seek Shade and Shelter:

- Create Shade: Use tarps, umbrellas, or natural cover like trees and rocks to protect yourself from direct sunlight.

- Cool Shelters: If possible, set up camp near water sources like rivers or lakes, which can provide a cooling breeze.

2. Hydrate Frequently:

- Drink Water Regularly: Sip water continuously throughout the day to stay hydrated. Avoid caffeinated and alcoholic beverages as they can lead to dehydration.
- Electrolytes: Include electrolyte solutions or sports drinks to replenish salts lost through sweating.

3. Wear Appropriate Clothing:

- Light and Loose: Wear lightweight, loose-fitting, and light-colored clothing to reflect sunlight and allow for airflow.
- Cover Up: Use wide-brimmed hats and sunglasses to protect your face and eyes. Long sleeves and pants can also protect your skin from sunburn.

4. Use Cooling Techniques:

- Wet Cloths: Dampen cloths or bandanas and place them on your neck, wrists, and forehead to cool down.
- Spray Bottles: Carry a spray bottle filled with water to mist yourself and create an evaporative cooling effect.

5. Plan Your Activities:

- Avoid Peak Heat: Schedule strenuous activities for early morning or late evening when temperatures are cooler.
- Rest Often: Take frequent breaks in the shade to prevent overheating.

How to Predict the Weather Without a Forecast

"Nature's whispers can tell you more about the weather than any forecast."

1. Observe the Sky:

- Cloud Types: Learn to identify different cloud types. For example, cumulonimbus clouds often indicate thunderstorms, while cirrus clouds can signal a change in the weather.
- Red Sky: A red sky at night suggests good weather the next day, while a red sky in the morning can indicate an approaching storm.

2. Pay Attention to Animal Behavior:

- Birds and Insects: Birds flying low or increased insect activity can indicate approaching rain.
- Animal Movements: Animals often become more active before a storm as they seek shelter.

3. Monitor Wind and Temperature:

- Wind Direction: Changing wind direction can indicate a shift in weather patterns. For example, a sudden shift to cold, northerly winds can suggest an incoming cold front.
- Temperature Changes: A rapid drop in temperature often precedes a storm.

4. Look for Dew and Fog:

- Dew Formation: Heavy dew or frost on the ground usually indicates clear skies and stable weather.

- Morning Fog: Fog in the morning typically clears up, leading to a sunny day.

"The sky and the animals around you are the best weather forecasters you could ever have."

Crazy Facts

Predictive Frogs:

Frogs are known to croak louder and more frequently before it rains. Their croaking is a way to attract mates, which they are more successful at when the air is moist.

Bees and Thunderstorms:

Bees return to their hives shortly before heavy rain or thunderstorms. They can sense changes in humidity and air pressure, prompting them to seek shelter to protect their hive.

Shark Weather Sense:

Sharks can detect changes in barometric pressure, which is why they often move to deeper waters before a storm hits. This behavior helps them avoid rough surface waters during bad weather.

Surviving Lightning Storms Outdoors

Lightning storms can be incredibly dangerous when you're caught outside. Here are steps to protect yourself:

1. Find Safe Shelter:

- Seek Enclosed Spaces: The safest place during a lightning storm is inside a fully enclosed building or a metal-topped vehicle.

- Avoid Small Shelters: Avoid open shelters, picnic pavilions, and tents as they do not provide adequate protection.

2. If Shelter is Unavailable:

- Stay Low: Move to lower ground to reduce the risk of being struck. Avoid hilltops, open fields, and isolated trees.
- Crouch Low: If you feel your hair stand on end (a sign that lightning is about to strike), crouch down with your feet together and hands over your ears to minimize ground contact. Do not lie flat on the ground.

3. Stay Away from Conductive Objects:

- Avoid Water: Do not swim or wade in water, and stay away from bodies of water.
- Metal Objects: Avoid carrying or being near metal objects such as backpacks with metal frames, trekking poles, or fences.

4. Spread Out:

- Group Safety: If you're with a group, spread out at least 20 feet apart to reduce the risk of multiple injuries from a single strike.

Making Snowshoes in the Wilderness

Imagine you and your friends are on a winter expedition through a remote, snowy forest. The snowfall has been relentless, and the snow is now several feet deep, making it nearly impossible to walk without sinking. As you struggle to move forward, it becomes clear that you need snowshoes to continue your journey. With no store in sight, you have to make them yourselves using the materials around you.

1. Gathering Materials:

You and your friends spread out to gather materials. You find a cluster of young, flexible saplings that are perfect for making the frames of your snowshoes. After cutting down the branches to the right size, you also gather some strong, thin vines to use as cordage. One of your friends finds a fallen tree with bark that can be stripped and used as additional cordage.

2. Forming the Frame:

Sitting around the campfire, you begin shaping the branches into oval frames. The branches are surprisingly pliable, and with some effort, you manage to bend them into shape. You and your friends work together to tie the ends of the branches securely, creating a sturdy frame for each snowshoe.

3. Creating the Webbing:

With the frames complete, you start weaving the cordage back and forth across the frame. It's a meticulous process, but soon the frames are filled with a crisscross pattern that will support your weight on the snow. Everyone helps to ensure the knots are tight and secure, knowing that any weakness could mean sinking into the deep snow.

4. Attaching Foot Straps:

Finally, you place your feet in the center of each snowshoe to mark where the straps should go. Using additional cordage, you tie straps across your feet and around your ankles, making sure they are snug but comfortable. You test the snowshoes, adjusting the straps as needed to ensure they stay securely in place.

As you strap on your homemade snowshoes and begin to walk, you're amazed at how well they work. You no longer sink into the snow with each step, making your journey through the forest much easier. The sense of accomplishment and teamwork lifts your spirits, and you continue your expedition with renewed energy.

5 Snowiest Places on Earth

1. Aomori City, Japan:

- Fact: Aomori City is known for its heavy snowfall, averaging over 312 inches (almost 26 feet) of snow each year. The city's unique geographical location between mountains and the Sea of Japan creates ideal conditions for significant snow accumulation.

2. Sapporo, Japan:

- Fact: Famous for its annual Snow Festival, Sapporo receives an average of 191 inches (almost 16 feet) of snow each winter. The city's snow sculptures and winter activities attract tourists from around the world.

3. Mount Baker, Washington, USA:

- Fact: Mount Baker holds the world record for the most snowfall in a single season, with an astounding 1,140 inches (95 feet) of snow during the 1998-1999 season. The mountain is a popular destination for skiing and snowboarding.

4. Valdez, Alaska, USA:

- Fact: Valdez averages about 326 inches (over 27 feet) of snow annually, making it one of the snowiest places in North America. The town's location near the Gulf of Alaska brings moisture-laden air that results in heavy snowfall.

5. Niseko, Japan:

- Fact: Niseko, located on Japan's northern island of Hokkaido, receives an average of 595 inches (almost 50 feet) of snow each year. The area's powdery snow and excellent ski conditions attract winter sports enthusiasts from all over the globe.

Surviving an Avalanche

Avalanches can occur suddenly, so knowing how to react is critical for survival.

1. Recognize Avalanche Signs:

- Warning Signs: Look for recent avalanche activity, cracking snow, and 'whumping' sounds. Pay attention to avalanche forecasts and advisories.

2. If Caught in an Avalanche:

- Yell and Signal: Shout to alert others and try to get their attention.
- Discard Heavy Gear: Drop heavy equipment like skis or backpacks to reduce weight and increase your mobility.

3. Create an Air Pocket:

- Cover Your Mouth: Use your hand or an item to cover your mouth and create an air pocket.
- Swim Motion: Try to stay on top of the snow using a swimming motion.

4. After the Avalanche Stops:

- Remain Calm: Try to stay calm and conserve energy.
- Create Space: If possible, use your hands to push away snow from your face and chest to create breathing room.
- Signal for Help: Use a whistle or call out periodically. Listen for rescuers and be prepared to make noise to assist them in locating you.

Crazy Avalanche Facts

The Deadliest Avalanche in History:

The deadliest avalanche on record occurred in 1970 in Peru, triggered by a massive earthquake. The avalanche from Mount Huascarán buried the town of Yungay and claimed approximately 20,000 lives. The scale of this disaster was so immense that it wiped out nearly the entire population of the town in minutes.

Avalanche at Wellington, Washington:

In 1910, the Wellington avalanche in Washington State, USA, became the deadliest avalanche disaster in U.S. history. Two trains were swept off the tracks, and the event resulted in the loss of 96 lives. The town of Wellington was later renamed Tye, partly to distance itself from the tragic event.

How to Make a Compass

A compass is an invaluable tool for navigation, but if you don't have one, you can make a simple version using common materials. This skill can help you find your way and stay on course in the wilderness.

"Finding north with a needle and leaf-simple science, vital skill."

The Solution: DIY Navigation

Making a compass involves creating a basic device that can indicate north using a magnetized needle. Here's

Gather Your Materials:

- You'll need a sewing needle, a small magnet or piece of steel wool, a leaf, and a cup or bowl of water.

Magnetize the Needle:

- Rub the needle with the magnet or steel wool about 30-50 times in one direction. This process aligns the needle's molecules, magnetizing it.

Prepare the Floating Platform:

- Place the leaf on the surface of the water, ensuring it floats freely. The water should be still and free of debris.

Assemble the Compass:

- Carefully place the magnetized needle on the leaf. The needle will align itself along the north-south axis, with the end you rubbed pointing north.

Use Your Compass:

- Once the needle settles, note the direction it points. Use this makeshift compass to navigate and find your way.

"A DIY compass: your guide when technology fails."

Ancient Invention:

- Did you know that the earliest known use of a compass dates back to the Han Dynasty in China around 206 B.C.? These early compasses were made of lodestone, a naturally magnetized mineral, and were primarily used for divination before their navigational potential was realized.

Navigational Revolution:

- The compass was crucial in the Age of Exploration. It allowed sailors to navigate the open seas with greater accuracy, leading to the discovery of new lands and sea routes. This revolutionized global trade and exploration during the 15th and 16th centuries.

Magnetic Declination:

- Did you know that a compass needle doesn't point exactly to the geographic North Pole? Instead, it points to the magnetic North Pole. The angle difference between geographic north and magnetic north is called magnetic declination, and it varies depending on where you are on Earth.

Compass Types:

- There are different types of compasses, including magnetic compasses, gyrocompasses, and electronic compasses. Magnetic compasses use Earth's magnetic field, while gyrocompasses and electronic compasses use technology to provide accurate directional information without relying on magnetism.

Space Navigation:

- Did you know that traditional magnetic compasses don't work in space because there's no significant magnetic field to align with? Astronauts and space explorers rely on gyroscopic and star-tracking systems to navigate in the vastness of space.

What to Do If You Get Lost

Getting lost in the wilderness can be a daunting experience, but staying calm and knowing what to do can turn a potentially dangerous situation into a manageable one.

The Solution: Stay Calm and Act

Reacting appropriately when lost involves staying calm and taking strategic steps to improve your situation. Here's what to do:

Stop and Stay Put:

- As soon as you realize you're lost, stop moving. Staying in one place increases the chances of being found by rescuers.

Think and Assess:

- Take a moment to calm yourself and assess your surroundings. Try to remember landmarks or the last known location.

Signal for Help:

- Use a whistle, mirror, or create a visible signal such as spelling out "HELP" with rocks or branches. Start a signal fire if it's safe to do so.

Stay Warm and Hydrated:

- Build a shelter to protect yourself from the elements. Find and purify water using available methods.

Wait for Rescue:

- Stay put and conserve your energy. Move only if you are certain of the direction to safety or to find better resources.

The Fun Fact: Did You Know?

Did you know that the survival rule of threes states you can survive three minutes without air, three hours without shelter in extreme conditions, three days without water, and three weeks without food? Prioritizing these needs can significantly increase your chances of survival.

Tying Essential Knots for Survival

Knots are more than just fancy rope tricks—they're essential survival skills. Whether you're building a shelter, securing gear, or rescuing a friend, knowing how to tie the right knot can make all the difference.

"A knot well-tied is a life well-secured."

The Solution: Knot Your Average Skill

Mastering essential knots involves practice and understanding their specific uses. Here's a guide to some must-know knots:

Gather Your Materials:

- Use rope, paracord, or even vines. Having a variety of cordage can be useful for different tasks.

Choose Your Knots:

- Focus on the square knot for joining two ropes, the bowline for creating a secure loop, and the clove hitch for attaching rope to a post or tree.

Practice Your Knots:

- Learn each knot step-by-step. Practice tying them in different situations to understand their strengths and weaknesses.

Apply Your Knots:

- Use the square knot to tie two ropes together securely. The bowline is perfect for rescue situations or securing a rope around yourself. The clove hitch is great for quickly securing a rope to a fixed object.

Test Your Knots:

- Make sure each knot is secure and can hold weight. Testing them in safe conditions ensures they'll perform well when needed.

"Every adventurer needs a few good knots in their toolkit."

Did You Know?

- The Oldest Known Knot: dates back to 5000 B.C.? Found in a fishing net in Denmark, this ancient knot shows that humans have relied on these simple yet effective tools for thousands of years.

- Topology explores the properties of knots and has applications in biology, chemistry, and physics.
- Record Breaker: Did you know that the world record for tying the fastest bowline knot is just 1.02 seconds? This knot-tying speed was achieved by a firefighter, showcasing the importance of knots in emergency services.
- Celtic Heritage: Did you know that Celtic knots, famous for their intricate, endless loops, were used in ancient Celtic art to symbolize eternity and interconnectedness? These knots are still popular in jewelry and designs today.
- Military Ties: Did you know that many knots used by the military, such as the square knot and the clove hitch, are essential for creating secure ties and lashing equipment together during operations?
- Knot Language: Did you know that in the Andes, the ancient Inca civilization used a system of knots called "quipu" to record information and communicate across their empire? These knots encoded data in a complex system of cords and colors.

Crossing a River Safely

Knowing how to cross a river safely is crucial to prevent accidents and stay dry.

"Rivers can be bridges or barriers–it's all in how you cross them."

The Solution: Safety First

Crossing a river safely involves careful assessment and technique. Here's what you need to do:

Assess the Situation:

- Look for the shallowest and widest part of the river to cross. Avoid areas with strong currents, deep water, or slippery rocks.

Prepare Yourself:

- Secure all your gear and use a walking stick or trekking pole to test the depth and stability of the riverbed. Wear sturdy footwear for better grip.

Use the Right Technique:

- Face upstream and cross at a slight angle, moving sideways. Keep your feet wide apart for better stability and use your stick to maintain balance.

Work as a Team:

- If you're with others, cross together by linking arms or holding onto a rope for extra stability. Move in unison to avoid slipping.

Stay Calm and Focused:

- Move slowly and deliberately. If the water becomes too strong, turn back and find another route.

"The key to river crossing: patience, balance, and respect for the current."

The Fun Fact: Did You Know?

Did you know that certain fish, like salmon, can leap up to 12 feet to cross obstacles in rivers? Their remarkable strength and determination remind us to approach river crossings with respect and caution.

"Every river crossed is a new story of adventure."

Making Rope from Plant Fibers

In a survival situation, having rope can be incredibly useful for building shelters, traps, or securing gear. If you don't have any with you, knowing how to make rope from plant fibers can be a lifesaver.

The Solution: Nature's Cordage

Making rope from plant fibers is a skill that transforms natural materials into strong, usable cordage. Here's

Gather Your Materials:

- Look for fibrous plants like nettles, dogbane, or the inner bark of certain trees. Harvest long strips of fiber from these plants.

Process the Fibers:

- Soak the fibers in water to make them more pliable. Once softened, split them into thinner strands by pulling them apart gently.

Twist and Weave:

- Twist two strands together tightly, then twist them around each other in the opposite direction. This process, known as reverse wrapping, creates a strong rope.

Continue the Process:

- Add more fibers as needed by overlapping the ends and continuing to twist and weave. This allows you to make rope of any length.

Test Your Rope:

- Once finished, test the strength of your rope by pulling on it and using it for various tasks. Ensure it can hold weight without breaking.

The Fun Fact: Did You Know?

Did you know that ancient Egyptians made rope from papyrus plants and palm fibers over 4,000 years ago? Their innovative use of natural materials helped build the pyramids and shows the enduring value of this simple technology.

Finding and Purifying Water Anywhere

Finding water becomes your top priority, but not just any water—safe, drinkable water. Knowing how to locate and purify water can turn a potentially perilous situation into a mere bump on your adventure trail.

"In the wilderness, water is life—find it, purify it, and every sip becomes a victory."

The Solution: Seek, Secure, and Purify

Locating Water:

- Look for signs of water such as vegetation, bird flights, or insect paths. Valleys and low-lying areas are natural collectors of rainwater and dew.

Collecting Dew:

- Using a cloth or bandana to absorb dew from grass and then wringing it into a container can be a lifesaver.

Purification Methods:

- Once you've found water, it's crucial to purify it. Boiling is the most reliable method. If you can't make a fire, use water purification tablets, or a portable water filter. Solar water disinfection (SODIS) can also be effective—filling a clear plastic bottle with water and leaving it in direct sunlight for 6 hours can kill most pathogens.

The Fun Fact: Did You Know?

- The largest organism on Earth is a fungus, Armillaria ostoyae, also known as the "humongous fungus," sprawling over 3.4 square miles in Oregon's Blue Mountains. But what's its link to water? This fungus, like many forms of life, thrives in moist conditions, illustrating nature's intricate relationship with water. This organism's sheer size reminds us of the importance of water in sustaining life in all its forms, from the smallest bacteria to the largest living networks. Plus, it's a fun tidbit to share around the campfire—as long as you're not foraging for mushrooms in the dark!

How to Build a Fire Without Matches

No need to worry! Humans have been making fire without modern conveniences for thousands of years, and with a bit of know-how, you can too.

The Solution: Let's Get Crackling

Creating fire without matches might sound like a task for wizards, but it's all about understanding the basics of friction, fuel, and air. Here are the steps to make your own fire, using only the natural resources around you:

Gather Your Materials:

- You'll need tinder (small, easily combustible materials like dry leaves, grass, or bark), kindling (small sticks), and fuel wood (larger sticks and logs).

Choose Your Method:

- There are a few matchless fire-making methods, such as the hand drill or the bow drill technique. Both involve spinning a stick rapidly between your hands, using another piece of wood as a base, to create enough friction to produce an ember.

Prepare Your Fire Bed:

- Clear a small area on the ground and create a nest for your ember using tinder. This is where your ember will catch and grow.

Get Spinning:

- Using your chosen method, work the drill until you create a glowing ember. This requires patience and steady effort, so don't get discouraged if it takes a few tries.

Transfer the Ember:

- Carefully place the ember into your tinder nest and gently blow on it to provide oxygen and encourage the flame. Once the tinder catches, add kindling, and then fuel wood to build your fire.

The Fun Fact: Did You Know?

Did you know that the world record for starting a fire with a hand drill is just under 3 seconds? That's faster than some people can light a match! While you might not be a world-record holder (yet!), mastering the skill of fire-making is not only a cool party trick but a valuable survival skill. Plus, there's something incredibly satisfying about starting a fire with your own two hands—it's like having a superpower.

Thank you Note

Thank you for reading "The End of the World: Survival Guide, Trivia, and Fact Book for the End of the World." Your journey through this guide shows your dedication to becoming a true survival expert. We hope you enjoyed the adventure and learned valuable skills along the way.

For exclusive free content, scan the QR code included. We would also greatly appreciate it if you could take a moment to leave a review on Amazon. Your feedback helps us continue to improve and provide you with the best possible reading experience.

Thank you once again for your support and happy surviving!